PERSONAL SERVICES

SECOND EDITION

Ferguson
An imprint of Infobase Publishing

Careers in Focus: Personal Services, Second Edition

Copyright © 2007 by Infobase Publishing

Ferguson
An imprint of Infobase Publishing
132 West 31st Street
New York NY 10001

Library of Congress Cataloging-in-Publication Data

Careers in focus. Personal services.—2nd ed.
    p. cm.
  Includes bibliographical references and index.
  ISBN 978-0-8160-6592-9 (hc : alk. paper) 1. Service industries—Vocational guidance—Juvenile literature. [1. Vocational guidance—Juvenile literature.] I. J.G. Ferguson Publishing Company. II. Title: Personal services.
  HD9980.5.C37 2007
  331.702—dc22
                              2006036243

Ferguson books are available at special discounts when purchased in bulk quantities for businesses, associations, institutions, or sales promotions. Please call our Special Sales Department in New York at (212) 967-8800 or (800) 322-8755.

You can find Ferguson on the World Wide Web at http://www.fergpubco.com

Text design by David Strelecky
Cover design by Ana Plé

Printed in the United States of America

MP MSRF 10 9 8 7 6 5 4 3 2 1

This book is printed on acid-free paper.

Table of Contents

Introduction

The service industry has made its way into almost every area of personal and business life, including image consulting, time management, productivity analysis, fitness training, and other arenas. Traditionally, the services provided were focused in such areas as marketing, public and media relations, business plan development, finances, productivity, automation, computer programming, and downsizing. Today, services sold have expanded beyond the business realm to include almost every possible aspect of modem life. You can find a consultant who will charge you a fee to help you plan your wedding, design and build your home, coordinate your wardrobe, walk or groom your dog, manage your finances, find an affordable college for your children, and place your parents in the right nursing home.

Some consultants in the service industry work independently out of their own home or office, and some work on a part- or full-time basis for consulting firms. Small, start-up businesses, mid-sized companies, large corporations, and governmental agencies frequently contract with consultants who have a specific area of business expertise. Individuals are increasingly seeking the assistance of consultants to assist them in their personal lives as well. Many consultants enter into short- or long-term contracts for their services, while others charge an hourly rate.

Some of the nontechnical personal services provided include fitness training, pet and home sitting, house cleaning, errand running, home maintenance repairs, and transporting children to activities. Repair services for items such as bicycles, lawn mowers, computers, small appliances, and televisions are also often home-based businesses.

The range of consulting possibilities is as endless as the imagination. People may operate repair, tailoring, tutoring, decorating, and food catering businesses out of their homes. They may consult and provide knowledge about home or office organization, perform home safety inspections, give advice on career advancement, or offer any other countless areas of expertise.

Because of the vast array of personal services offered, the structure of the industry varies considerably. There are, however, certain parallels that can be made across these broad areas. Individuals who work in any of the service fields need experience, expertise, self-motivation, and a general knowledge of business to succeed.

I

Consultants usually develop the skills they offer by working within the field—often in a number of different jobs—or using related work experience and translating it into new skills. The skills and the reputation of the consulting service are dependent on the level of competence and expertise that the owner of the business demonstrates. Consultants should develop a business plan that will help them establish, maintain, and market their businesses. Bankers or small business development consultants can usually help with the plan. If service consultants seek financing from a private or public source to fund their venture, business plans are almost always required.

Consultants must seek out clients or customers. This may be done through advertising, calling potential clients, asking previous or current clients for referrals, or other promotional methods. In personal services, it is essential that workers continually solicit new business while servicing current clients. As their reputation develops, it becomes easier to maintain clients, and, as a result, referrals from satisfied clients increase. It is vital that consultants keep up on news and changes within the field so that the services offered are the most current.

Managing a service-based business has all of the same elements as managing a standard business, even if it is only a one-person enterprise. Salary, staff, profits, marketing, communications, and taxes must all be handled professionally. Questions regarding expansion, services offered, and fees must be addressed periodically.

The home-based consultant must have the ability to work independently, possess good time-management skills, and be self-motivated. Self-employed people often work more than 40 hours a week and rarely have a nine to five job. Running an independent business or consulting service can be very tiring and time consuming; however, the work can be very rewarding when it succeeds. Some of the drawbacks cited by self-employed individuals include isolation from other workers, uncertain workflow and resulting income, and lack of benefits. Self-employed workers should realize that they will have to pay their own health, life, and disability insurance. Vacation time and sick days are not paid and actually may produce a negative effect on income.

Pay for service providers ranges from minimum wage to a hefty hourly rate or substantial contract pay. Usually the rate depends on the service offered, area of expertise, experience, and reputation. The law of supply and demand can be a factor as well. The best way to determine the going rate for a specific service is to visit with people who either market or hire the service.

Professional organizations can usually provide general rate guidelines as well. The service industry is currently quite strong. There may be future fluctuations in certain areas of consulting and business services, but the overall need for professionals and nonprofessionals that can be hired on a temporary, as-needed basis will continue to exist.

As companies downsize and cut back on costs, they tend to outsource some of their work to consultants and small-business owners. This way, companies can hire the expertise needed, when needed, and avoid committing to any long-term contracts or benefits. Similarly, as layoffs occur in certain industries and job security is no longer a sure thing, the prospect of being your own boss and controlling your own fate is becoming more appealing to a growing population. The option of traveling to another room in your home instead of fighting rush-hour traffic appeals to many burned-out professionals. The increased use of computers, faxes, modems, and the Internet has opened up the possibility of working from home to individuals around the world.

The opportunities for professional and nonprofessional services are expected to grow significantly in response to our fast-paced world and the decreased amount of time people have to care for children, cook, run errands, and handle their financial affairs. In addition, people are becoming more willing to pay for these services, either as a necessity or a luxury.

Each article in *Careers in Focus: Personal Services* discusses a particular personal-services-related career in detail. The articles appear in Ferguson's *Encyclopedia of Careers and Vocational Guidance,* but have been updated and revised with the latest information from the U.S. Department of Labor, professional organizations, and other sources. The following paragraphs detail the sections and features that appear in the book.

The **Quick Facts** section provides a brief summary of the career including recommended school subjects, personal skills, work environment, minimum educational requirements, salary ranges, certification or licensing requirements, and employment outlook. This section also provides acronyms and identification numbers for the following government classification indexes: the Dictionary of Occupational Titles (DOT), the Guide to Occupational Exploration (GOE), the National Occupational Classification (NOC) Index, and the Occupational Information Network (O*NET)-Standard Occupational Classification System (SOC) index. The DOT, GOE, and O*NET-SOC indexes have been created by the U.S. government; the NOC index is Canada's career classification system. Readers can use the identification numbers listed in the Quick Facts section to access further information about a career. Print editions of the DOT (*Dictionary of Occupational Titles.* Indianapolis, Ind.: JIST Works, 1991) and GOE (*The Complete Guide for Occupational Exploration.* Indianapolis, Ind.: JIST Works, 1993) are available at libraries. Electronic versions of the NOC (http://www23.hrdc-drhc.gc.ca) and O*NET-SOC (http://online.onetcenter.org) are available on the Internet. When no DOT, GOE, NOC, or O*NET-SOC numbers are present, this means that the U.S. Department of Labor or Human Resources Development Canada have not created a numerical designation for this career. In this instance, you will see the acronym "N/A," or not available.

The **Overview** section is a brief introductory description of the duties and responsibilities involved in this career. Oftentimes, a career may have a variety of job titles. When this is the case, alternative career titles are presented. The **History** section describes the history of the particular job as it relates to the overall development of its industry or field. **The Job** describes the primary and secondary duties of the job. **Requirements** discusses high school and postsecondary education and training requirements, any certification or licensing that is necessary, and other personal requirements for success in the job. **Exploring** offers suggestions on how to gain experience in or knowledge of the particular job before making a firm educational and financial commitment. The focus is on what can be done while still in high school (or in the early years of college) to gain a better understanding of the job. The **Employers** section gives an overview of typical places of employment for the job. **Starting Out** discusses the best ways to land that first job, be it through the college placement office, newspaper ads, or personal contact. The **Advancement** section describes what kind of career path to expect from the job and how to get there. **Earnings** lists salary ranges and describes the typical fringe benefits. The **Work Environment** section describes the typical surroundings and conditions of employment—whether indoors or outdoors, noisy or quiet, social or independent. Also discussed are typical hours worked, any seasonal fluctuations, and the stresses and strains of the job. The **Outlook** section summarizes the job in terms of the general economy and industry projections. For the most part, Outlook information is obtained from the U.S. Bureau of Labor Statistics and is supplemented by information taken from professional associations. Job growth terms follow those used in the *Occupational Outlook Handbook*. Growth described as "much faster than the average" means an increase of 27 percent or more. Growth described as "faster than the average" means an increase of 18 to 26 percent. Growth described as "about as fast as the average" means an increase of 9 to 17 percent. Growth described as "more slowly than the average" means an increase of 0 to 8 percent. "Decline" means a decrease by any amount. Each article ends with **For More Information,** which lists organizations that provide information on training, education, internships, scholarships, and job placement.

Careers in Focus: Personal Services also includes photographs, informative sidebars, and interviews with professionals in the field.

Bodyguards

OVERVIEW

Bodyguards, sometimes called *personal protection officers* or *personal security workers,* protect their clients from injury, kidnapping, harassment, or other types of harm. They may guard a politician during a political campaign, a business executive on a worldwide trip, a movie star going to the Academy Awards, or anyone else who wants personal protection. Bodyguards may be employed by a government agency, by a private security firm, or directly by an individual.

Bodyguards work in potentially dangerous situations and must be trained to anticipate and respond to emergencies. They may carry weapons. Bodyguards combine the ability to react quickly and expertly in a tense or dangerous situation with the ability to predict, prevent, or avoid many of these situations.

HISTORY

People, especially rich and powerful people, have always needed protection. Whether a CEO visiting an overseas plant or a Roman senator meeting with various plaintiffs in a legal case, people who made important decisions or controlled large sums of money always had guards whom they could trust by their side.

As security demands became more complex, the role of bodyguards evolved and expanded. No longer was it enough to simply know how to use a gun or to be particularly adept at martial arts. Bodyguards were expected to help devise strategies to avoid problem situations. They used new surveillance techniques, planning strategies, and other tactics to anticipate possible dangerous situations.

QUICK FACTS

School Subjects
Physical education
Psychology

Personal Skills
Following instructions
Helping/teaching

Work Environment
Indoors and outdoors
Primarily multiple locations

Minimum Education Level
Some postsecondary training

Salary Range
$22,330 to $50,000 to
$70,000+

Certification or Licensing
Recommended

Outlook
About as fast as the average

DOT
372

GOE
04.02.02

NOC
6651

O*NET-SOC
33-9032.00

In recent times bodyguards have become involved in many different types of situations. Rock stars or movie stars hire bodyguards to protect themselves against being mobbed by overzealous fans. Executives of large corporations are also likely to enlist the aid of a bodyguard to protect against possible kidnapping or other types of harm. Bodyguards often accompany their clients overseas because police in other countries might not be able to provide the type of security the clients have come to expect. Bodyguards often drive their clients from place to place while on assignment.

THE JOB

Although a bodyguard's ultimate responsibility is relatively straightforward—to protect a client from danger—there are a wide variety of tasks involved in this assignment. Bodyguards are part personal aide and part police officer. As personal aides, bodyguards help plan and implement schedules; as police officers, they protect their clients at public or private events. They often act in their client's business and publicity interests, as well; stories of camera-snatching bodyguards have become common fodder for the gossip pages.

Bodyguards face possible danger whenever they are on duty. When there was an attempted assassination of President Ronald Reagan in March 1981, for example, his Secret Service bodyguards quickly shielded the president with their own bodies as gunshots were fired. Bodyguards may have to sacrifice their own security in defense of those they are hired to protect. Of course, bodyguards are not just sitting targets. They are trained to react appropriately in any situation, life-threatening or not. Skilled bodyguards do all they can to minimize danger to those they are protecting, as well as to themselves. As a result of their careful preparation, bodyguards carry out most assignments relatively uneventfully.

By keeping a watchful eye on their clients, bodyguards are able to avoid many possible problems. In many cases, people are not actually out to harm a client but are simply interested in meeting an important person. Bodyguards learn not to overreact to these encounters, and in most cases, a polite warning eliminates any potential problem.

When a client hires a bodyguard for a specific event, the bodyguard will determine how many additional people may be needed to provide adequate protection. The client's schedule and travel arrangements will be coordinated for maximum security and, if the client is appearing at a public event, the bodyguard will become familiar with the location, especially the exits and secured areas, in case the client needs sudden and immediate protection from danger.

A bodyguard opens the car door for an executive of a Fortune 500 company. *(Jim McGuire, Index Stock Imagery)*

Bodyguards often work in tandem with other security people as part of a large security operation. For example, bodyguards may help develop a plan to safeguard a major politician who is giving a speech, while *security guards* develop a plan to safeguard the building where the speech will take place. All security personnel meet to discuss overall arrangements to ensure that specific details are worked out. Typically, one person will coordinate the security operations.

Bodyguards are hired to protect their clients, and activities that infringe on this job must be avoided. At an awards ceremony, for example, a bodyguard must keep an eye on the client and not gawk at celebrities. Bodyguards should not confuse the glamour and excitement of an assignment with self-importance. Indeed, it is the person who can remain calm in the midst of an exciting event and can sense possible danger when all eyes are elsewhere who makes a skillful bodyguard.

REQUIREMENTS

High School
Since bodyguards must be prepared for any possibility, the more skilled and knowledgeable they are in a range of areas, the better the protection they can offer someone. If you are interested in becoming

a bodyguard, in high school you should take courses in a variety of subjects, including psychology, English, and especially physical education.

Postsecondary Training

Bodyguards often begin their careers in civilian law enforcement or the military, where they learn the necessary skills of crowd control, use of weapons, and emergency response. Those wanting to become a security professional working for a government agency, such as the U.S. Department of State, will need to complete a bachelor's degree. Generally, bodyguards have some higher education, although a college degree is not always necessary. A well-educated person can often be the most responsive to rapidly changing situations, and, of course, work in crowd psychology, law, and criminal justice can help a bodyguard better understand the demands of the job. On-the-job experience with different types of people in stressful situations is an integral part of the training. Depending on the employer, new hires may also need to complete between several weeks to several months of training covering topics such as criminal law, use of firearms, personal protection techniques, and first aid.

Certification or Licensing

Certification, while not required, will enhance your professional image in the eyes of potential employers. ASIS International administers the certified protection professional program. Applicants must have a certain amount of educational or professional experience and pass a multiple choice exam focusing on eight areas of security management: security principles and practices, business principles and practices, personnel security, physical security, information security, emergency practices, investigations, and legal aspects. Other certifications offered by ASIS International include the physical security professional designation and the professional certified investigator designation.

Other Requirements

Since many bodyguards are former police officers, bodyguards generally must be above the minimum age for police officers. This minimum age varies from 18 to 21, depending on the city or state. If a bodyguard comes from the police ranks, he or she must also have passed a thorough physical exam. Many bodyguards also begin their careers as security guards or as other types of security personnel, for which they receive special training. Other bodyguards come from a military background or have worked for government agencies such as the Secret Service.

Excellent physical fitness is a requirement for a bodyguard. Despite a popular image of bodyguards as big and tough men, and despite the fact that larger men can serve as deterrents, extreme physical strength is not an absolute requirement and many women have made successful careers as bodyguards. It is much more important that a bodyguard combine intelligence, sensitivity, and bravery with the ability to act quickly and decisively. The ability to blend into a crowd is also helpful.

Many bodyguards receive training in martial arts, and increasingly they are incorporating the study of counterintelligence operations, electronic security devices, and surveillance techniques. Bodyguards often have training in first aid. Many bodyguards are also trained in specialized defensive driving techniques that enable them to maintain better control of a vehicle in emergency situations. However, being a bodyguard is not carte blanche to engage in action-movie heroics. Bodyguards must understand the appropriate use of force, especially since they can be arrested—or sued—for going over the line.

Bodyguards who travel to foreign countries must be well versed in the language and culture of the host country. Good verbal skills are vital, and a bodyguard must be able to communicate directions to people at all times. A bodyguard must also be aware of what to expect in any situation. That is why an understanding of the customs of a certain area can help the bodyguard perceive unusual events and be alert for possible problems. Similarly, the legal use, registration, and licensing of weapons differs from country to country, and the bodyguard who travels to foreign countries needs to be familiar with the regulations governing weapons in the country in which he or she is working.

Since bodyguards often work with important people and around sensitive information, they may be required to take a lie detector test before they begin work. Background checks of their work and personal histories may also be required. Bodyguards who work as permanent employees of a client must also exercise discretion and maintain confidentiality. Bodyguards should have a keen eye for detail and be able to spot trouble long before it happens. This ability to anticipate problems is crucial. A good bodyguard should rarely have to stop a kidnapping attempt as it occurs, for example, but should rather prevent the attempt from happening through a combination of careful planning and skilled observation. If action is needed, however, the response must be swift and effective.

EXPLORING

Because bodyguards must be mature and highly skilled, it is difficult to obtain real opportunities to explore this career while still in high school. Nevertheless, you can take classes and talk to people to get a feel for the demands of the profession. Classes in criminal justice should give an indication of the challenges involved in protecting people. Talking to a police officer who works part time as a bodyguard is another good way to learn about opportunities in this field. Many police departments hire high school students as police trainees or interns, providing an excellent introduction to careers in security and law enforcement.

Without the requisite skills and experience, it is difficult to get summer work as a bodyguard. It may be possible, however, to work in some other capacity at a security firm that hires bodyguards and in this way interact with bodyguards and learn more about the day-to-day rewards and challenges of the profession.

EMPLOYERS

Bodyguards can find work with private security firms and government agencies. Politicians, performing artists, actors, and other individuals in the public eye who need personal protection also employ bodyguards.

STARTING OUT

Many people begin a career as a bodyguard on a part-time basis; for example, police officers often take on assignments while off-duty from police work. The reason that most of them start on a part-time basis is that the police training they receive is ideal preparation for work as a bodyguard. In addition to the excellent training a police officer receives, the officer is often in a good spot to receive job offers. Someone looking for a bodyguard may call the local police station and ask if there are officers willing to take on an assignment. Then, as a person acquires greater experience as a bodyguard and more and more people know of the person's skills and availability, additional work becomes available. That person may then work full-time as a bodyguard or continue on a part-time basis.

Military service may also provide the background and skills for entry into this field. Many bodyguards enter this career after service in one of the Special Forces, such as the Green Berets or the Navy SEALs, or after experience in the military police. Other bodyguards enter this field through a career with private security companies and often begin training while employed as security guards. Careers with the Secret Service, the Federal Bureau of Investigation, or other government police and intelligence agencies may also provide the necessary background for a career as a bodyguard. In fact, a successful history with one of these respected agencies is one of the most attractive factors for potential employers.

ADVANCEMENT

Those who enter the field as part-time bodyguards may soon find full-time work. As bodyguards develop their skills and reputation, private security firms or government agencies may hire them. They may be given additional training in intelligence operations, surveillance techniques, and the use of sophisticated firearms.

Some bodyguards find opportunities as *personal protection and security consultants*. These consultants work for private companies, evaluating personal security operations and recommending changes. They may begin their own security services companies or advance to supervisory and director's positions within an existing company.

EARNINGS

Many bodyguards begin their careers on a part-time basis and earn between $25 and $50 per hour for routine assignments. These assignments might last several hours. Earnings for full-time bodyguards vary enormously, depending on factors such as the guard's experience, the notoriety or prestige of the client, the type of assignment, and whether the bodyguard is employed directly by the client or through a security agency. Highly dangerous, sensitive, or classified assignments generally pay more than do routine protective assignments. Training in special skills, such as electronic surveillance, also brings higher wages. According to findings by the Economic Research Institute, bodyguards just starting out in the field earn an average salary of approximately $22,330. Those with five years of experience average approximately $27,570 annually, and those with 10 years of experience average approximately $31,400. Depending on the bodyguard's employer, earnings may be higher than these. For example, in 2006, Distinguished Domestic Services, a placement agency for domestic professionals, reported on its Web site (http://distinguisheddomestics.com) that personal protection officers could expect a salary range of $40,000 to $70,000 annually. The agency also notes that these security personnel have usually had some type of government training. The Bureau of Diplomatic Security of the U.S. Department of State reported a starting salary range for its special agents in security of $37,413 to $51,788 in 2006.

Bodyguards employed by private security firms may receive health and life insurance benefits and other benefits. Benefits vary for those employed by private clients. Bodyguards who work as part of a government agency receive health and life insurance, vacation, holiday, and sick leave pay, and a pension plan. Self-employed bodyguards must provide their own insurance.

WORK ENVIRONMENT

A bodyguard goes wherever the client goes. This means that the job can be physically demanding. Bodyguards must also have the strength and coordination to take actions to protect the client if the situation warrants it. A bodyguard must be able to act swiftly and decisively to thwart any attempt to harm a client.

Bodyguards must be willing to risk their own safety to protect their clients. They should be comfortable handling firearms and using physical means of restraining people.

Since bodyguards must accompany their clients at all times, there is no set work schedule. Bodyguards often work highly irregular hours, such as late evenings followed by morning assignments. It is also not unusual to work weekends, since this is when many high-profile clients make public appearances. Travel is a frequent component of the job.

OUTLOOK

Opportunities for bodyguards are likely to be strong as more and more people look for protection from an increasing number of threats such as stalkers, terrorists, and violent demonstrators. In addition, the threat of kidnapping and terrorism is always present for politicians, celebrities, business leaders, and others who enjoy wide recognition, and these individuals will take steps to safeguard themselves and their families by hiring bodyguards. As more and more companies enter the global economy, their business will take their executives to more areas of social and political unrest, and companies will need to increase their efforts for protecting their employees.

Government agencies will continue to hire bodyguards, but much of the growth in employment will take place in the private sector. Many bodyguards will find work with private security companies. Some estimates suggest that employment in private security may nearly double over the next decade.

Those with the most skill and experience will enjoy the best employment prospects. While the majority of bodyguards continue to be men, the increasing use of advanced security technologies will open up more and more opportunities for women.

FOR MORE INFORMATION

For information on security careers and certification, contact
ASIS International
1625 Prince Street
Alexandria, VA 22314-2818
Tel: 703-519-6200
Email: asis@asisonline.org
http://www.asisonline.org

For more information on the Bureau of Diplomatic Security and the U.S. Department of State, visit this agency's Web site.
Bureau of Diplomatic Security
U.S. Department of State
Washington, DC 20522-2008
http://www.state.gov/m/ds

Your local Secret Service field office or headquarters office can provide more information on becoming a special agent. To learn more about secret service work, find career fairs, and get contact information for field offices, visit the agency's Web site.
U.S. Secret Service
Washington, DC 20001
Tel: 202-406-8000
http://www.treas.gov/usss

Caterers

QUICK FACTS

School Subjects
Business
Family and consumer science

Personal Skills
Artistic
Helping/teaching

Work Environment
Primarily indoors
Primarily multiple locations

Minimum Education Level
Some postsecondary training

Salary Range
$15,000 to $35,000 to
$75,000

Certification or Licensing
Voluntary (certification)
Required by certain states
(licensing)

Outlook
About as fast as the average

DOT
319

GOE
09.05.02

NOC
N/A

O*NET-SOC
N/A

OVERVIEW

Caterers plan, coordinate, and supervise food service at parties and at other social functions. Working with their clients, they purchase appropriate supplies, plan menus, supervise food preparation, direct serving of food and refreshments, and ensure the overall smooth functioning of the event. As entrepreneurs, they are also responsible for budgeting, bookkeeping, and other administrative tasks.

HISTORY

Catering is part of the food service industry and has been around for as long as there have been restaurants. Once viewed as a service available only to the very wealthy, many people now use catering for various types of gatherings.

THE JOB

A caterer is a chef, purchasing agent, personnel director, and accountant. Often a caterer will also play the role of host, allowing clients to enjoy their own party. A caterer's responsibilities vary, depending on the size of the catering firm and the specific needs of individual clients. While preparing quality food is a concern no matter what the size of the party, larger events require far more planning and coordination. For example, a large catering firm may organize and plan a formal event for 1,000 people, including planning and preparing a seven-course meal, decorating the hall with flowers and wall hangings, employing 20 or more wait staff to serve food, and arranging the entertainment. The catering firm will also set up the tables and chairs and provide the necessary linen, silverware, and dishes. A catering company may organize 50 or so such events a month or only several a year. A smaller catering organization may concentrate on simpler events, such as preparing food for an informal buffet for 15 people.

Caterers service not only individual clients but also industrial clients. A caterer may supervise a company cafeteria or plan food service for an airline or cruise ship. Such caterers often take over full-time supervision of food operations, including ordering food and other supplies, supervising personnel and food preparation, and overseeing the maintenance of equipment.

Caterers need to be flexible in their approach to food preparation, that is, able to prepare food both on- and off-premises, as required by logistical considerations and the wishes of the client. For example, if the caterer is handling a large banquet in a hotel or other location, he or she will usually prepare the food on-premises, using kitchen and storage facilities as needed. The caterer might also work in a client's kitchen for an event in a private home. In both cases, the caterer must visit the site of the function well before the actual event to determine how and where the food will be prepared. Caterers may also prepare food off-premises, working either in their own kitchens or in a mobile kitchen.

Working with the client is obviously a very important aspect of the caterer's job. Clients always want their affairs to be extra special, and the caterer's ability to present such items as a uniquely shaped wedding cake or to provide beautiful decorations will enhance the ambiance and contribute to customer satisfaction. The caterer and the client work together to establish a budget, develop a menu, and determine the desired atmosphere. Many caterers have their own special recipes, and they are always on the lookout for quality fruits, vegetables, and meats. Caterers should have an eye for detail and be able to make fancy hors d'oeuvres and eye-catching fruit and vegetable displays.

Although caterers can usually prepare a variety of dishes, they may have a specialty, such as Cajun or Italian cuisine. Caterers may also have a special serving style (for example, serving food in Renaissance period dress) that sets them apart from other caterers. Developing a reputation by specializing in a certain area is an especially effective marketing technique.

The caterer is a coordinator who works with suppliers, food servers, and the client to ensure that an event comes off as planned. The caterer must be in frequent contact with all parties involved in the affair, making sure, for example, that the food is delivered on time, the flowers are fresh, and the entertainment shows up and performs as promised.

Good management skills are extremely important. The caterer must know how much food and other supplies to order, what equipment will be needed, how many staff to hire, and how to coordinate various activities to ensure a smooth-running event. Purchasing the proper supplies entails knowledge of a variety of food products, their suppliers, and the contacts needed to get the right product at the best possible price.

Caterers working in a large operation may appoint a manager to oversee an event. The manager will take care of the ordering, planning, and supervising responsibilities and may even work with the client.

As entrepreneurs, caterers have many important day-to-day administrative responsibilities, such as overseeing the budgeting and bookkeeping of the operation. They must make sure that the business continues to make a profit while keeping its prices competitive. Additionally, caterers must know how to figure costs and other budgetary considerations, plan inventories, buy food, and ensure compliance with health regulations.

Caterer helpers may prepare and serve hors d'oeuvres and other food and refreshments at social functions, under the supervision of the head caterer. They also help arrange tables and decorations and then assist in the cleanup.

REQUIREMENTS

High School

Does working as a caterer sound interesting to you? If so, you should take home economics or family and consumer science classes in high school. Any class that will teach you about food preparation, presentation, and nutrition will be valuable. Since caterers run their own businesses, you should also take math, accounting and bookkeeping, and business classes to prepare for dealing with budgets, record keeping, and management. Like so many small business owners today, most caterers will use computers for such things as planning schedules, keeping addresses, and updating accounts, so be sure to take computer classes. English classes will help you to hone your communication skills, which will be essential when you deal with customers. Finally, round out your education by taking health and science classes, which will give you an added understanding of nutrition, how the body works, and how to prevent food contamination.

Postsecondary Training

The best way to enter the catering industry is through a formal training program. One way of obtaining this education is to attend a vocational or community college with an appropriate program. Many of these schools and colleges offer professional training in food science, food preparation, and catering. Often these programs will provide opportunities for students to work in apprentice positions to gain hands-on experience.

As the catering field has grown more competitive, many successful caterers are now choosing to get a college degree in business administration, family and consumer science (home economics), nutrition, or a related field. If you decide to get a four-year college degree, make sure your course work includes subjects in nutrition, health, and business management, regardless of your major. A number of colleges and universities also offer assistance to their students in finding apprenticeships. The Foundation of the National Association of Catering Executives (NACE) provides information on universities and colleges offering programs relevant to those interested in the catering profession.

Certification or Licensing

As a measure of professional status, many caterers become certified through the NACE. To qualify for this certification, called the certified professional catering executive (CPCE), caterers must meet certain educational and professional requirements as well as pass a written examination. To keep their certification current, caterers must also fulfill requirements such as completing continuing education courses and attending professional conferences. The International Food Service Executives Association also offers the certified food executive, the certified food manager, and other certification designations. Applications are available online; see the Web site listed at the end of the article for more information.

Most states require caterers to be licensed, and inspectors may make periodic visits to catering operations to ensure that local health and safety regulations are being maintained in food preparation, handling, and storage.

Other Requirements

The professional caterer should have a commitment to learning. Foods go in and out of fashion, new techniques develop, and our understanding of nutrition and health is always growing. The successful caterer will want to keep up with these new developments in the field. Because caterers run their own businesses, they should be organized, able to work on tight schedules, and conscientious about keeping accurate records. The successful caterer enjoys working with people and also has an artistic eye, with the ability to arrange food and settings in an appealing manner.

EXPLORING

One relatively simple way for you to begin exploring your interest in catering is to do some cooking at home. Make dinner for your family once a week, try out a new recipe for muffins, or bake cookies for your friends. If people enjoy your creations, you may be able to offer catering services to them when they have parties.

If your high school has a club for those interested in home economics, join it. You'll meet other people with similar interests and may find others with whom to cook. Some organizations, such as 4-H, offer programs about food preparation and careers in food service. Find out if there is such a group in your area and join it as well.

Another great way to explore food service is through service work. Volunteering in the kitchen of a local homeless shelter where you can help prepare meals for large numbers of people can provide a great experience, both for your professional ambitions and for humanitarian reasons.

Learn More About It

Arduser, Lora, and Douglas Robert Brown. *The Professional Caterer's Handbook: How to Open and Operate a Financially Successful Catering Business.* Ocala, Fla.: Atlantic Publishing Company, 2005.

Bode, Sony. *Successful Catering: Managing the Catering Operation for Maximum Profit.* Ocala, Fla.: Atlantic Publishing Company, 2002.

Brown, Amy. *Understanding Food: Principles and Preparation* 2nd ed. Belmont, Cal.: Brooks Cole, 2003.

Labensky, Sarah R., and Alan M. Hause. *On Cooking: A Textbook of Culinary Fundamentals* 3rd ed. Upper Saddle River, N.J.: Prentice Hall, 2002.

Marriott, Norman G., and Robert B. Gravani. *Principles of Food Sanitation* 5th ed. New York: Springer, 2006.

Vivaldo, Denise. *How to Start a Home-Based Catering Business* 5th ed. Guilford, Conn.: Globe Pequot Press, 2005.

Finally, get part-time or summer work at a local restaurant. Even if you end up working at an ice cream parlor when what you really want to do is cater eight-course meals, you'll still gain valuable experience working with food, money, and customers.

EMPLOYERS

Most caterers own their own businesses and are, therefore, self-employed. Caterers, however, do have many different types of clients. Individuals may need catering services for a party or special family celebration. Industrial clients, such as company cafeterias, airlines, country clubs, schools, banquet halls, cruise ships, and hotels, may require catering services on a large scale or at regular intervals.

STARTING OUT

Some caterers enter the profession as a matter of chance after helping a friend or relative prepare a large banquet or volunteering to coordinate a group function. Most caterers, however, begin their careers after graduating from college with a degree in a program such as home economics or finishing a culinary training program at a vocational school or community college.

Qualified individuals can begin working as a manager for a large catering firm or as a manager for a hotel or country club or banquet service. Those most likely to start a catering business will have extensive experience and sufficient finances to purchase equipment and cover other start-up costs.

ADVANCEMENT

As with most service-oriented businesses, the success of a caterer depends on the quality of work and a good reputation. Well-known caterers can expand their businesses, often growing from a small business to a larger operation. This may mean hiring assistants and buying more equipment in order to be able to serve a larger variety of clientele. Caterers who initially worked out of their own home kitchens may get an office or relocate to another area in order to take advantage of better catering opportunities. Sometimes successful caterers use their skills and reputations to secure full-time positions in large hotels or restaurants as banquet coordinators and planners. Independent caterers may also secure contracts with industrial clients, such as airlines, hospitals, schools, and corporations, to staff their cafeterias or supply food and beverages. They may also be employed by such companies to manage their food operations.

EARNINGS

Earnings vary widely, depending on the size and location of the catering operation and the skill and motivation of the individual entrepreneur. Many caterers charge according to the number of guests attending a function. In many cases, the larger the event, the larger the profit. Earnings are also influenced by whether a caterer works full time or only part time. Even very successful caterers often work part time, working another job either because they enjoy it or to protect themselves against a possible downturn in the economy.

Full-time caterers can earn between $15,000 and $60,000 per year, depending on skill, reputation, and experience. An extremely successful caterer can easily earn more than $75,000 annually. A part-time caterer may earn $7,000 to $15,000 per year, subject to the same variables as the full-time caterer. Because most caterers are self-employed, vacations and other benefits are usually not part of the wage structure.

WORK ENVIRONMENT

A caterer often works long hours planning and preparing for an event, and the day of the event might easily be a 14-hour workday, from setup to cleanup. Caterers often spend long hours on their feet, and although the work can be physically and mentally demanding, they usually enjoy a great deal of work flexibility. As entrepreneurs, they can usually take time off when necessary. Caterers often work more than 60 hours a week during busy seasons, with most of the work on weekends and evenings, when events tend to be scheduled.

There is a lot of variety in the type of work a caterer does. The caterer must work closely with a variety of clients and be able to adapt to last-minute changes. Caterers must be able to plan ahead, work gracefully under pressure, and have the ability to adapt to last-minute mishaps. Attention to detail is critical, as is the ability to work long hours under demanding situations. They must be able to direct a large staff of kitchen workers and waitpersons and be able to interact well with clients, guests, and employees.

OUTLOOK

The U.S. Department of Labor projects that employment opportunities in food service should continue to grow at an average rate through 2014. Opportunities will be good for individuals who handle special events, such as weddings, bar and bat mitzvahs, and other festive occasions less affected by downswings in the economy. On the other hand, events such as business functions may offer less catering opportunities during times of recession and cutbacks.

Competition is keen as many hotels and restaurants branch out to offer catering services. Despite competition and fluctuating economic conditions, highly skilled and motivated caterers should be in demand throughout the country, especially in and around large metropolitan areas.

FOR MORE INFORMATION

For information on scholarships, student branches, certification, and industry news, contact
International Food Service Executives Association
304 West Liberty, Suite 201
Louisville, KY 40202-3035
Tel: 502-583-3783
http://www.ifsea.com

For information on certification programs and catering publications, contact
National Association of Catering Executives
9881 Broken Land Parkway, Suite 101
Columbia, MD 21046-3015
Tel: 410 290 5410
http://www.nace.net

For more information on programs and chapters, contact
National 4-H Council
7100 Connecticut Avenue
Chevy Chase, MD 20815-4934
Tel: 301-961-2800
Email: info@fourhcouncil.edu
http://www.fourhcouncil.edu

For education information, visit the following Web site:
Foundation of the National Association of Catering Executives
http://www.nacefoundation.org

Color Analysts and Image Consultants

School Subjects
Art
Business
Theater/dance

Personal Skills
Artistic
Communication/ideas

Work Environment
Primarily indoors
Primarily multiple locations

Minimum Education Level
Some postsecondary training

Salary Range
$13,400 to $20,610 to
$100,000+

Certification or Licensing
Recommended

Outlook
About as fast as the average

DOT
N/A

GOE
N/A

NOC
N/A

O*NET-SOC
N/A

OVERVIEW

Color analysts assess their clients' coloring, including skin tone and hair and eye color, and teach them how to use their most flattering colors in clothing and makeup. Image consultants usually work with people in business, helping them present themselves in a professional manner.

Color and image consultants offer programs for individual women or men, for professional or social organizations, or for all the employees of one company. Some work with retailers, teaching salespersons about color and style and presenting in-store workshops.

HISTORY

In their book, *Color Me Beautiful's Looking Your Best,* Mary Spillane and Christine Sherlock cite a study by Albert Mehrabian. He found that the impression we make on others is made up of 55 percent appearance and behavior, 38 percent speech, and only 7 percent the content of what we say. These figures clearly show the importance of presenting yourself well in business, social, and other settings. Beauty consultants have been around for some time, but their work is constantly evolving. Because our society is increasingly mobile, and we change jobs more often than our parents did, we are constantly establishing ourselves with new groups. In addition, television has increased our awareness of appearance and what it tells us about the individual. Projecting a positive image through our appearance and behavior helps us gain acceptance

22

from social and business contacts, fit into the workplace, and meet the public.

In 1980, with the publication of Carole Jackson's book, *Color Me Beautiful,* many people, especially women, began to think of what they purchased and wore in a different way. No longer willing to accept whatever fashion decreed, they wanted colors and styles that enhanced their individual appearance. By the time more than 20 million people had read this *New York Times* bestseller, clothing manufacturers, cosmetic companies, and retailers felt the impact of the new consumer demand.

In the meantime, other businesses were dealing with their increased need for employees with technological backgrounds. Such employees often were totally involved in the technical aspects of their work and unconcerned about the impression they made on coworkers, clients, and the general public. Many companies began to provide training to help employees project better images, increasing the demand for image consultants.

THE JOB

Most color and image consultants are entrepreneurs, meaning that they own and manage their businesses and assume all of the risks. They may work with individuals, groups, or both. Christine Sherlock, director of training and communications for Color Me Beautiful, reports that her firm trains color analysts in color and its use in wardrobe and makeup Those who wish to become image consultants take additional training so they can help clients work on their overall appearance and grooming, as well as improve their voices, body language, and etiquette. Consultants also may learn to coach clients on dealing with the public and the media.

Susan Fignar, president of S. Fignar & Associates Inc., is a corporate image trainer and consultant who has been quoted in *Cosmopolitan,* the *Wall Street Journal,* and the *Chicago Tribune.* She works with some of the country's largest corporations and offers a variety of corporate programs and interactive workshops. Fignar says she provides training that helps people bring out their best personal and professional presence. Like other entrepreneurs, her business requires constant sales and marketing to obtain clients.

Her training sessions deal with such topics as making a good first impression, everyday etiquette, developing self-esteem and confidence, verbal communication, body language and facial expression, overall appearance, and appropriate dress for every occasion. She notices an increasing demand for her services in dress code consulting and training sessions on business casual dress.

Sherlock says consultants get satisfaction from helping others look better and feel good about themselves. "When a consultant helps a client with her wardrobe," she says, "the client not only saves money; she uses 100 percent of her wardrobe and no longer complains she has nothing to wear."

REQUIREMENTS

High School

If you are interested in this work, you will benefit from taking classes and being involved in activities that develop your ability to communicate and increase your understanding of visual effects. Helpful classes to take include English, speech, and drama. Activities to consider participating in include drama clubs and debate teams. In drama club you may have the opportunity to help apply makeup, select wardrobes, and learn about the emotional impact appearances can have. Art classes, especially those that teach color theory, are also beneficial. Since many people in this line of work are entrepreneurs, consider taking any business, bookkeeping, or accounting classes that will give you the skills to run your own business.

Any part-time job working with the public is valuable. You can gain excellent experience from selling clothing or cosmetics in department stores, from working in beauty salons or spas, or from working as a waitperson. Volunteer work that involves working with people will also help you hone your people skills.

Postsecondary Training

There are no formal, standardized training programs for color analysts and image consultants. In general, Susan Fignar recommends attending seminars or classes on color, psychology, training methods, and communications. She adds that a degree in liberal arts, with a major in education, is a plus for those working at the corporate level.

Color Me Beautiful has trainers who travel throughout the country. They offer people who wish to become consultants basic classes in skin care, makeup, and color analysis, and advanced classes in such subjects as theory of style and presentation. Most classes take one or two days for a single topic; most working consultants take at least one new class each year.

If you get to know a color analyst or image consultant personally, you may be able to arrange an informal internship of your own.

Some people begin their careers in this field by working as apprentices to other consultants. Color Me Beautiful accepts a two-month apprenticeship with an approved consultant.

Certification or Licensing
The Association of Image Consultants International (AICI) provides three levels of certification: first level certification, certified image professional, and certified image master. Contact the AICI for more information.

Other Requirements
Christine Sherlock recommends this field for those who like to work with and help other people and says an interest in fashion and style are also obviously very helpful. A general flair for art and design would prove useful. Analysts and consultants should be friendly, outgoing, supportive of others, able to offer constructive feedback, and open to change. There are few disabilities that would prevent an individual from doing this work.

Susan Fignar believes experience in the business world, especially in management and public contact, is essential for corporate consulting. She says that corporate consultants must be mature, poised, and professional to have credibility, and that people are usually between the ages of 33 and 40 when they enter this field.

EXPLORING

One way to explore this career is to arrange for a personal visit to a consultant. The AICI, for example, offers lists of qualified consultants throughout the country (see the end of this article for contact information).

There are several books you can read to learn more about color and image consulting. Sherlock recommends *Color Me Beautiful* by Carole Jackson (Ballantine Books, 1987), *Color Me Beautiful's Looking Your Best: Color, Makeup, and Style* by Mary Spillane and Christine Sherlock (Madison Books, 2002), and *Women of Color* by Darlene Mathis (Capital Books, 1999). Fignar recommends *Image Consulting: The New Career* by Joan Timberlake (Acropolis Books, 1983), which discusses the various areas in which image consultants specialize. Because networking is so important in getting clients, she also suggests *Networlding: Building Relationships and Opportunities for Success* by Melissa Giovagnoli (John Wiley & Sons, 2001). Local libraries should have additional books on color, fabrics, style, etiquette, and body language.

EMPLOYERS

For the most part, color analysts and image consultants are self-employed. They run their own consulting businesses, which allows them the freedom to decide which image consulting services they wish to offer. For example, some consultants concentrate on working with corporate clients; other consultants may also advise individuals. Consultants may get the products they sell from one company, such as Color Me Beautiful, or they may offer a range of products and services that provide ways for clients to feel good about themselves. Those in apprenticeships and consultants just entering the field may work for consultants who have already established their businesses.

STARTING OUT

Some consultants enter the field through apprenticeships. Fignar began by working in advertising, where she had extensive experience in meeting planning and often was responsible for company visitors. She eventually attended a training program on fashion and image consulting. She says there are many routes to entering this field.

ADVANCEMENT

Workers can advance from color analysts, to image consultants, to trainers by gaining experience and additional education. Sherlock began as an apprentice and has advanced through various positions with Color Me Beautiful. Salon and department store employees would advance along the path their employers have laid out.

Fignar hopes to expand her business by adding new clients, taking advantage of new trends, developing training for future image consultants, and forming alliances with consultants who offer related services. This is par for the course for all self-employed analysts and consultants. She has had her own business for seven years and says it takes three to five years to get a corporate consulting business established.

EARNINGS

A color analyst's or image consultant's earnings are determined by the number of hours the consultant works, the type of clientele, and the consultant's location. Christine Sherlock says earnings are highest in New York City and southern California. Some consultants increase their incomes by offering additional services. Susan Fignar estimates that earnings start at under $20,000 but can reach $75,000 or more for top performers. Since many color analysts and image consultants own their own businesses, it may also be helpful to consider that some small business owners may earn only about $15,000 a year, while the most successful may make $100,000 or more. The U.S. Department of Labor reports that median annual earnings for beauticians and cosmetologists were $20,610 in 2005, with 10 percent making $13,400 or less and 10 percent making $37,380 or more.

Sherlock points out such advantages as owning your own business, flexible hours, controlling your own time, and opportunity for personal growth and development. Because most consultants are self-employed, they must provide their own insurance and other benefits.

WORK ENVIRONMENT

Many consultants work out of their homes. Color consultants also work in salons, boutiques, day spas, and retail areas. The work is indoors and may involve travel. Sherlock comments that the work has changed her life and that she loves everything she has done in the field.

Fignar works at corporate sites and training facilities, speaks before various organizations, and has appeared on radio and television. She has contact with management and with human resources and training departments. Her work schedule has busy and slow periods, but she usually works from 40 to 50 hours a week and sometimes makes evening presentations. She describes her work as exciting, draining, and full of time constraints.

OUTLOOK

The employment of personal appearance workers is expected to grow as fast as the average through 2014, according to the *Occupational Outlook Handbook,* mainly due to increasing population, incomes, and demand for cosmetology services.

Christine Sherlock says the economy has little effect on color consulting. During sluggish times, people still want the lift that such beauty services give them. The demand for consultants is growing steadily, and she believes self-employed people with successful businesses aren't likely to be out of work. The field is evolving, with new opportunities in corporate work.

Susan Fignar says corporate consultants are affected by downsizing because when companies cut personnel they also reduce training. "Right now," she says, "the field is growing." She says the hot topics are casual dress for business, etiquette, communications, and public image. Fignar feels security comes from constantly working to build your consulting business. She advises consultants to develop a 60-second sales pitch so they're always ready to describe their services to any prospective client they meet.

FOR MORE INFORMATION

This organization has information on continuing education, mentorship programs, and certification.

Association of Image Consultants International
431 East Locust Street, Suite 300
Des Moines, IA 50309-1999
Tel: 515-282-5500
Email: info@aici.org
http://www.aici.org

This company provides information on contacting local consultants. Check out its Web site for information on their products.

Color Me Beautiful
http://www.colormebeautiful.com

Dry Cleaning and Laundry Workers

OVERVIEW

Dry cleaning and laundry workers dry clean, wash, dry, and press clothing, linens, curtains, rugs, and other articles made from natural and synthetic fibers. This work is done for individuals, families, industries, hospitals, hotels, schools, and other institutions. In smaller laundries and dry cleaning plants, one worker may perform several different tasks. In larger plants, however, a worker usually performs only one job in the cleaning process. Some dry cleaning and laundry workers specialize in one or two aspects of the process. Today, the industry has a national sales volume of over $5 billion annually. Over 216,000 people are employed nationwide in this industry.

Dry cleaners and laundries range from small independent businesses that service families and the community to large wholesale and institutional plants. Many institutions such as hospitals, prisons, and hotels have their own laundry facilities on site.

HISTORY

In the 19th century, machines were invented to agitate and wring out clothes, followed by automatic washing and drying machines. As the number of hospitals, schools, factories, and other businesses increased, the need to have textile items continually cleaned also increased. Institutional laundries sprang up to fulfill these institutions' needs for fresh sheets, towels, uniforms, and other articles.

Also in the late 19th century, the first synthetic fabric, nitrocellulose rayon, was invented. Eventually hundreds of different synthetic fabrics were invented. These new fabrics called for additional cleaning techniques. Items that would lose their shape or color in water needed to be cleaned with chemical solvents. Even some natural fibers were found to last longer and retain their appearance better when cleaned with chemicals. Dry cleaning stores, employing specially trained workers, were thus established. As needs and lifestyles changed, the dry cleaning and laundering industries have had to adapt their services to meet the consumers' demands. In addition, there is an ongoing need to develop, test, and introduce new cleaning chemicals and processes, as well as to invent more efficient machinery.

THE JOB

Dry cleaning and laundry workers' responsibilities vary depending on the type and size of the facility that employs them. Duties can range from store clerk to delivery driver to becoming involved in any or all of the dry cleaning and pressing process. Many times in smaller laundries and dry cleaning plants, workers may be required to perform several different tasks. In larger plants, the worker may have the opportunity to become specialized in certain procedures or duties. In some facilities there may be the possibility to supervise or manage the processes, although many industries require a college degree to advance to this level.

Sales route drivers are often employed to pick up and deliver laundry and dry cleaning to homes and businesses. Some people bring their laundry to the dry cleaning facilities. Here, *sales clerks* take the items from customers, add up the cleaning costs, and fill out cleaning tickets or receipts. Some clerks may be required to use a computer to do these tasks. Clerks also inspect the articles for rips and stains, mark the items to identify the customer to whom they belong, and bundle them for cleaning.

In the cleaning plant, *markers* put tags on articles so they are not lost. Then they send the items to rooms where they are either dry cleaned or laundered. If the articles are to be dry cleaned, *classifiers* sort them according to the treatment they need. If the items are to be laundered, *sorters* may weigh the items and put individual customer's articles into net bags to keep them together.

Laundry and dry cleaning spotters brush stains with chemicals or other cleaners to remove the stains. Plants that clean rugs may employ *rug measurers* to record the size of the rugs so they can be stretched back to their original size after cleaning.

A dry cleaning worker inputs an order into a computer. *(Katie Deits, Index Stock Imagery)*

When articles are ready to be cleaned, *laundry laborers* and *loaders* take the laundry to the washing machines. *Washing machine operators* then wash the articles. When the washing cycle is complete, these operators load the laundry into extractors. Extractors are machines that remove about 50 percent of the water from washed laundry. The damp laundry is then put onto a conveyor belt that takes it to dryers, conditioners, and other machines.

Dry cleaners operate the machines that use chemicals to clean the items. *Hand dry cleaners* clean by hand delicate items that need individual attention.

When items are dry or semidry, *pressers* or *finishers* operate machines that use heat or steam to press the items. *Silk finishers* work on delicate items. *Flatwork finishers* feed linens into automatic pressing machines. *Puff ironers* press portions of garments that cannot be ironed with a flat press by pulling them over heated metal forms.

REQUIREMENTS

High School
In most shops, laundry and dry cleaning workers learn their skills on the job. The only requirement is usually a high school diploma or its equivalent. Computers are being used more and more in this industry, so computer familiarity is a plus. High school courses that

might be helpful include chemistry, computers, textiles, machine shop, sewing, and clothing construction.

Other Requirements

Large plants may offer formal and specialized training programs. Spotters may take as long as two years to learn their trade completely because they must learn how different chemicals react with different fabrics and dyes. Finishers and dry cleaners can learn to do their jobs skillfully in under a year.

Another way to learn dry cleaning and laundry skills is through various trade associations that provide newsletters and seminars. The International Fabricare Institute and the National Cleaners Association, which operates the New York School of Dry Cleaning, offer many courses and seminars and also publish journals, newsletters, and bulletins to help workers learn new skills and techniques.

Workers need to be in good health since they are on their feet most of the day and may need to lift heavy bundles. They should enjoy working with their hands and with machines, and should have good eyesight and manual dexterity. They must also be dependable, fast workers who can follow orders and handle repetitive tasks. Workers who meet with customers should be friendly and have good communication skills.

EXPLORING

To find out more about laundry and dry cleaning work, students may arrange to visit a plant or institution and talk with owners and workers. Students may try obtaining part-time or summer employment in the field to further explore these types of jobs. Libraries are also a good source of information about this industry, as is contacting the sources at the end of this article.

EMPLOYERS

Laundry or dry cleaning positions are available nationwide, in small communities and large cities. Typical employers range from community dry cleaners and laundries to large institutions such as hotels, motels, hospitals, nursing homes, prisons, some government facilities, and commercial industries.

STARTING OUT

If you are interested in laundry or dry cleaning positions, contact state or local employment offices or read newspaper want ads to find job leads. Checking the Yellow Pages for local dry cleaners or laundries may provide some job contacts. The best way to find work, however, is to apply directly to dry cleaning or laundry plants.

ADVANCEMENT

Workers in dry cleaning and laundry jobs generally advance by learning their basic assignments and moving to more skilled tasks. Skilled workers may be promoted to line supervisors or department heads, for example. Employers may also send promising employees to programs offered by trade associations to enhance their skills. Advancement in these jobs is generally limited, however.

Motivated workers may become plant managers after several years of experience. Many businesses, though, prefer to hire college graduates with degrees in management for these positions.

EARNINGS

Entry-level pay for dry cleaning and laundry workers is often not much more than minimum wage. The U.S. Department of Labor reported a median hourly wage of $8.38 for dry cleaning and laundry workers in 2005. This hourly wage translates into a yearly income of roughly $17,440 for full-time work. Salaries ranged from less than $13,160 to more than $25,580.

Workers receive time-and-a-half for working overtime and may receive slightly higher, regular wages for working night shifts. Some plants award bonuses to fast workers, and many sales route workers earn commissions. Some employers provide medical insurance, pension plans, vacations, and paid holidays. These workers generally work 35 to 40 hours a week, although the number of hours available may fluctuate with the amount of work.

WORK ENVIRONMENT

Dry cleaning plants and laundries are clean, well lighted, and ventilated to remove fumes. The work is hot, however, even with adequate ventilation. Most laundry and dry cleaning workers are on their feet all day. In addition, lifting large bundles of clothing can be hard work.

Workers stand near machines whose noise and heat may be annoying. They may occasionally suffer burns from the hot equipment. Many of the chemical solvents used are toxic and require cautious handling. Other chemicals may cause allergic reactions or irritations of the skin, lungs, or eyes.

Work schedules may vary depending on the facility. Some larger institutions may require shift work.

OUTLOOK

The U.S. Department of Labor expects overall employment of textile, apparel, and furnishings workers to decline through 2014. It makes no specific predictions, however, for dry cleaning and laundry workers. The general trends in the textile and apparel industries will not necessarily affect the large number of dry cleaning establishments in the country or the need for laundry workers in hotels, hospitals, and nursing homes. In the next 10 years, automation advances will cut the number of unskilled and semiskilled workers needed, and most openings will be for skilled workers, drivers, and managers. In the dry cleaning industry, many opportunities exist for workers who can perform pressing and spotting procedures. Job prospects look best for workers who are versatile and who have a good knowledge of textiles.

FOR MORE INFORMATION

For information on careers and schooling in laundry work and dry cleaning, contact
> **International Fabricare Institute**
> 14700 Sweitzer Lane
> Laurel, MD 20707-5903
> Tel: 800-638-2627
> Email: techline@ifi.org
> http://www.ifi.org

For information on careers in dry cleaning and education courses available, contact
> **National Cleaners Association**
> 252 West 29th Street
> New York, NY 10001-5271
> Tel: 800-888-1622
> http://www.nca-i.com

For more information on the dry cleaning, laundry, and fabrics industry, visit the following Web site:
> **Cleaners Online**
> http://www.cleanersonline.com

Funeral Home Workers

OVERVIEW

The *funeral director,* also called a *mortician* or *undertaker,* handles all the arrangements for burial and funeral services of the deceased, in accordance with family's wishes. This includes the removal of the body to the funeral home, securing information and filing for the death certificate, and organizing the service and burial plans. The director also supervises the personnel who prepare bodies for burial. An *embalmer* uses chemical solutions to disinfect, preserve, and restore the body and employs cosmetic aids to simulate a lifelike appearance. A *mortuary science technician* works under the direction of a funeral director to perform embalming and related funeral service tasks. Most are trainees working to become licensed embalmers and funeral directors.

Funeral home workers are employed throughout the world in small communities as well as large metropolitan areas. Because cultures and religions affect burial customs, funeral home workers must be sensitive and knowledgeable to these differences.

There are approximately 30,000 funeral directors and 8,700 embalmers employed in the United States.

HISTORY

Since the beginning of civilization, funeral ceremonies have been held both to honor the dead and to help mourners in their grief. In all cultures, people have dealt with the mystery of death by means of rituals and

QUICK FACTS

School Subjects
Biology
Business
Psychology

Personal Skills
Helping/teaching
Leadership/management

Work Environment
Primarily indoors
One location with some
  travel

Minimum Education Level
Some postsecondary training

Salary Range
$22,520 to $47,630 to
  $89,990+

Certification or Licensing
Required

Outlook
More slowly than the
  average

DOT
338

GOE
11.08.01

NOC
6272, 6683

O*NET-SOC
11-9061.00, 39-4011.00,
39-4021.00

ceremonies, often burying significant objects with their dead to aid them in their afterlife.

Embalming was practiced by the Egyptians as early as 4000 B.C. Bodies were covered with a dry powdered substance, called natron, soaked in a soda solution, rubbed with oil and spices (and sometimes tar and pitch), and finally wrapped in linen. Mummies preserved in this manner have remained intact to this day.

Modern methods of embalming were developed in the 18th century in Europe. Precise anatomical knowledge and the development of standardized chemical preparations and new synthetic materials enable the embalmer to restore the appearance of the deceased to a condition approximating life.

Funerals, like all ceremonies, are intimately related to the society in which they occur. As society has changed, so have funerals. Emphasis in funeral customs in the United States has undergone a shift in recent years from a preoccupation with the dead to a concern for the living. Today, men and women in the funeral service industry are concerned with the emotional and physical well-being of the survivors. This shift in attitude has amounted to an increased need for sensitivity and empathy in funeral home workers.

THE JOB

Funeral directors are responsible for all the details related to the funeral ceremony and burial. The law determines some of their tasks, such as compliance with sanitation and health-related standards. Other responsibilities are administrative and logistical, such as securing information and filing the death certificate. Finally, custom and practice dictate some tasks.

Directors handle all the paperwork that needs to be filed, such as the death certificate, obituary notices, and may even assist the family in applying for the transfer of insurance policies, pensions, or other funds.

They assist the family of the deceased in the choice of casket, type of funeral service, and preparation of the remains, which may be burial, cremation, or entombment. Part of the director's job is to be a caregiver and, at times, a counselor. They must deal respectfully and sympathetically with families of the deceased, guiding them through decisions they may not be prepared to make and taking great care that their wishes are carried out.

First, the funeral director arranges for the body to be transported to the funeral home. The director then makes complete arrangements for the funeral ceremony, determining first the place and time of the service. If there is to be a religious ceremony, it is the director's responsibility to contact the appropriate clergy. Directors oversee the selection and playing of music, notify pallbearers, and arrange the placement of the casket and floral displays in the viewing parlor or chapel. If a service is held in the funeral home, the director arranges seating for guests. After the service, the director organizes the procession of cars to the cemetery, or wherever arrangements have been made for the disposal of remains. Funeral directors may have to make arrangements for transporting a body to another state for burial.

Most directors are also trained, licensed, and practicing embalmers. Embalming is a required sanitary process done to the body within 24 hours of death to preserve the remains for burial services. If a body is not being autopsied, it is brought to a funeral home where it is washed with a germicidal soap. The body is placed in a lifelike position, and an incision is made in a major artery and vein where a tube pumps a preservative and disinfectant solution through the entire circulatory system. Circulation of the chemical solution eventually replaces all blood with the embalming fluid. In addition, embalmers remove all other gases and liquids from the body, replacing it with disinfectant chemicals for preservation.

The preparation of an autopsied body can be much more complex, depending on the condition of the deceased. The embalmer may repair disfigured parts of the body and improve the facial appearance, using wax, cotton, plaster of paris, and cosmetics. When the embalming process is complete, the body is dressed and placed in a casket.

Mortuary science technicians assist directors and embalmers in the funeral home. They are usually involved in a training process that will ultimately lead to a job as a licensed funeral director, embalmer, or both. Technicians may assist in various phases of the embalming process. Since embalming fluids are available in different chemical compositions and color tints, learning the various formulas is one important part of the technician's job. The technician may also be responsible for helping in the application of cosmetics to the body to create a natural, lifelike appearance. It is important that they use the proper products and techniques for applying them, since the result must satisfy and comfort those who view the body. (In some funeral homes, a licensed cosmetologist, called a *mortuary cosmetologist*, may perform these cosmetic services.) After the cosmetic application is complete, the technician may assist with the dressing and placement of the body for the funeral service. Finally, the technician may be responsible for cleaning the embalming area and equipment in accordance with required standards of sanitation.

Funeral home workers carry a casket to a grave site. *(Jim Whitmer Photography)*

Mortuary science technicians may also perform duties related to the actual funeral service. They may prepare the casket for the service and transport it to the cemetery. They also assist in receiving and ushering mourners to their seats at the service, organizing and managing the funeral procession, or any other tasks that are necessary for the occasion.

REQUIREMENTS

High School
If you are interested in entering the field of mortuary science, consider taking classes in algebra, chemistry, biology, physics, and any other laboratory courses available. In addition, a psychology class might be helpful since funeral home workers must deal with distraught families and friends of deceased persons.

Postsecondary Training
Almost all states require funeral service practitioners to have completed postsecondary training in mortuary science varying from nine months to four years. Several colleges and universities now offer two- and four-year programs in funeral service. The American Board of Funeral Service Education accredits about 55 mortuary sci-

ence programs. A typical curriculum at a school of mortuary science would include courses in anatomy, embalming practices, funeral customs, psychology, accounting, and public health laws. Laboratory study is essential in many of the courses and can account for up to a quarter of the program.

After completion of at least a two-year program, the graduate can apply to work as a mortuary science technician. Graduates who want to obtain a license in either embalming or funeral directing must work as an apprentice in an established funeral home for one to three years, depending on the state's requirements. Some schools of mortuary science have arrangements with local area funeral homes to provide students with either a work-study program or a period of school-supervised funeral service work (residency or apprenticeship).

Certification or Licensing

All states require embalmers and funeral directors to be licensed. Some states grant a combination single license covering the activity of both the embalmer and funeral director. In order to maintain licensure, a growing number of states require continuing education classes.

After successfully completing their formal education, including apprenticeship, prospective funeral service practitioners must pass

Did You Know?

- There are more than 21,500 funeral homes in the United States. They employ more than 103,250 workers.
- Approximately 11 percent of all funeral homes are owned by five publicly traded stock corporations.
- Fifty-one percent of funeral service graduates are women.
- About 67 percent of funeral service graduates today have no prior family connection to the funeral business.
- The percentage of people choosing cremation as their final form of disposition is expected to increase by more than 20 percent by 2025.
- The average cost of a funeral in July 2004 was $6,500.
- The National Funeral Directors Association, the world's largest funeral service organization, was founded in 1882.

Sources: American Board of Funeral Service Education, National Funeral Directors Association

a state board examination that usually consists of written and oral tests and demonstration of skills. Those who wish to practice in another state may have to pass that state's examination as well, although some states have reciprocity arrangements to waive this requirement.

Other Requirements

A strong sense of understanding, empathy, and a genuine desire to help people at a time of great stress are essential qualities for anyone wanting to work at a funeral home. Workers must be tactful and discrete in all contacts with the bereaved family and friends. Funeral service workers must always be compassionate and sympathetic, but also remain strong and confident to accomplish the necessary tasks of the job. Funeral home workers must also be good listeners. For example, when details such as cosmetics and clothing are discussed, they must be especially attentive to the client's wishes.

The work sometimes requires physical strength for lifting the deceased or their caskets. Good coordination is also needed to perform the precise procedures used in embalming, restoration, and cosmetology.

EXPLORING

Ask your high school guidance counselor for information on mortuary science or check out your public and school library for useful books, magazines, and pamphlets. Local funeral homes are the most direct source of information. Arrange a visit with a funeral director and embalming staff to learn about the nature of the work and the importance and intricacies of funeral service. After becoming acquainted with local funeral homes, ask around to see if you can work part time, either handling clerical or custodial duties. Finally, check out the organizations listed at the end of this article for more career information.

EMPLOYERS

Funeral directors are usually employed by a funeral home or are in the business themselves. There are about 30,000 funeral directors in the United States, approximately 20 percent of whom are self-employed. The majority of embalmers and mortuary science technicians are also employed by funeral homes, though a small amount work for hospitals and medical schools. Employers for these professions are located worldwide.

STARTING OUT

After attending an accredited school of mortuary science for two to four years, beginning workers start out as mortuary science technicians, working under the supervision of licensed directors or embalmers.

Most mortuary science schools provide placement assistance for graduates. Additionally, since many schools require internship programs, students are often able to obtain permanent jobs where they have trained.

ADVANCEMENT

For many years, most funeral homes were family businesses. Younger members of the family or their husbands or wives were expected to move up into managerial positions when the older members retired. This is changing, however, as the majority are entering the field today having no prior background or family connection. Therefore, the potential for advancement into managerial positions is considerably greater than in the past.

The natural progression in the field is from mortuary science technician to fully licensed embalmer, funeral director, or both. With licensing comes more opportunity for advancement. While many people who enter this field aspire to eventually own their own funeral homes, there are other possibilities as well. One advanced specialty, for example, is that of *trade embalmers,* who embalm under contract for funeral homes. Their work typically includes restorative treatment. Also, an increasing number specialize in selling funeral and burial arrangements in advance. Providing the option to make plans ahead of time can give clients peace of mind. Finally, with sufficient financial backing, funeral service practitioners may establish their own businesses or purchase a portion, or all, of an existing one.

The percentage of mortuary science graduates who pursue advancement outside the funeral home is small, but opportunities do exist. Funeral supply manufacturers employ licensed funeral service personnel because of their familiarity with the products and their ability to handle technical problems. Workers may be employed in customer relations or product sales.

EARNINGS

Salaries of funeral home workers vary depending on experience, services performed, level of formal education, and location. According to the U.S. Department of Labor, the median annual salary for funeral directors was $47,630 in 2005. The lowest paid 10 percent earned less than $27,670, and the highest paid 10 percent earned more than $89,990 a year. The department also reports that embalmers earned a median annual salary of $36,960 in 2005. Salaries ranged from a low of $22,520 for the lowest paid 10 percent to a high of $59,420 or more per year for the highest paid 10 percent.

According to the American Board of Funeral Service Education, starting salaries for new funeral service licensees often closely approximate those of starting teachers in the same community.

In some metropolitan areas, many funeral home employees are unionized; in these cases, salaries are determined by union contracts and are generally higher than regions in which employees have not organized a union.

Benefits may vary depending on the position and the employer.

WORK ENVIRONMENT

In firms employing two or more licensees, funeral workers generally have a set schedule of eight-hour days, five or six days a week. Because services may be needed at any hour of the day or night, though, shifts are usually arranged so that someone is always available at night and on weekends.

In smaller firms, employees generally work long hours at odd times and often remain on call and within a short distance of the funeral home. Some may work in shifts, such as all days one week and all nights the next. Occasionally, overtime may be necessary.

Employees who transport bodies and accompany the funeral procession to the cemetery are frequently required to lift heavy weights and to be outdoors in inclement weather. Sometimes directors and embalmers must handle the remains of those who have died of contagious diseases, though the risk of infection, given the strict sanitary conditions required in all funeral homes, is minimal.

In this field, much of workers' time is spent trying to help families work through their grief. Because they are exposed daily to such intense emotion, as well as death and sometimes unpleasant or upsetting sights, there is the chance that the work may be depressing or emotionally draining. Employees need to be aware of that possibility and be able to approach situations philosophically and with a clear head.

Many who enter this field find that their occupation can be very rewarding because the work they do may help the family and friends of the deceased adjust at a time when they are greatly stressed by grief. They help provide an essential social service and one that, when well done, brings comfort and satisfaction.

OUTLOOK

Employment for funeral directors should grow more slowly than the average for all occupations 2014. But the need to replace those retiring (more directors are 55 or older than in other occupations) or leaving the profession will spur a demand for newly trained directors.

Despite this demand, there are a limited number of employers in any geographical area, and it might be wise for prospective students to check with employers in their area to see what the chances for employment will be. If possible, students should try to arrange post-graduate employment while they are still in school.

Job security in the funeral service industry is relatively unaffected by economic downturns. Despite the flux and movement in the population, funeral homes are a stable institution. The average firm has been in its community for more than 40 years, and funeral homes with a history of over 100 years are not uncommon.

FOR MORE INFORMATION

For information on careers in the funeral service industry, colleges that offer programs in mortuary science, and scholarships, contact
American Board of Funeral Service Education
3432 Ashland Avenue, Suite U
St. Joseph, MO 64506 1333
Tel: 816-233-3747
http://www.abfse.org

Visit the NFDA's Web site to read the career brochure Thinking about a Career in Funeral Service?
National Funeral Directors Association (NFDA)
13625 Bishop's Drive
Brookfield, WI 53005-6607
Tel: 800-228-6332
Email: nfda@nfda.org
http://www.nfda.org

Household Movers

OVERVIEW

Household movers pack and load furniture and other household belongings into moving vans, drive the vans to new locations, and unload the contents. Movers often unpack and set up items according to the customer's specifications. Before the move, they may prepare inventories that describe the condition of the items they are transporting, and then, check that the items are undamaged after the move.

Household movers are often hired to move home and business furniture. Sometimes movers are employed by retail furniture and appliance dealers to deliver items purchased by consumers and businesses.

HISTORY

Until recently, most people did not move very often. Once settled, individuals tended to stay in the same area for much of their lives. A family might move to a different address in the same town, but long-distance moves and multiple moves in a short span of years were unusual. It was around the beginning of the 20th century, when the automobile began its transformation of American life, that families became less stationary. The trend toward more frequent moving continues to this day.

In recent decades especially, shifting factors in local and national economies have created many attractive new jobs across the United States while other jobs have faded in importance and desirability. These new job opportunities, together with inexpensive, easily available transportation, have spurred many people to uproot themselves from their old homes to seek a better life. Individuals and families also make major moves for other reasons, such as to attend a particular school, to live in a more pleasant climate, or to live closer to friends or relatives.

As our society became more mobile, the need arose for professional moving assistance. Few individuals or families have access to a vehicle large enough to transport an entire home. Household movers transport our beds, carpets, dishes, clothes, and the almost infinite variety of things we need or cherish. For many people facing life in new surroundings, the ability to keep necessary and personal items can help provide comfort and a sense of continuity while adjusting to a move.

THE JOB

Household movers do more than simply load and unload furniture in and out of a moving van. Much of their job revolves around planning and preparing for the move. Before any items are moved, the individual who is in charge (usually the driver) goes through the house to determine the order in which the household goods should be loaded on the truck. Larger, heavier items are usually put in first to utilize space efficiently and avoid stacking heavy pieces on top of less sturdy ones.

Before they pack items, movers may make an inventory list of everything that is to be moved, noting the condition of each item. They pay special attention to any existing damage to furniture and delicate objects in order to avoid potential disputes over damages made during the move. The customer receives a written copy of the inventory.

Van drivers oversee the packing and loading of items into the moving van or truck, drive to the specified destination, and supervise the unloading and unpacking, according to the client's specifications. *Local drivers* work in a set geographic area in which moves can be completed in one day. *Linehaul drivers* are employed for long-distance moves that take more than one day to complete. Drivers need to be skillful operators of large vehicles; they often have to maneuver into tight spots or back up to loading areas. They are responsible for inspecting the moving truck before and after trips, preparing regular reports on its condition, and keeping a daily log. Van drivers may be responsible for the vehicle's routine maintenance services, either by sending it to a mechanic or by doing necessary repairs themselves. Drivers also see that the inventories of the truck contents are completed properly. They collect payment or obtain a signature from the customer and resolve various difficulties arising from the move.

Moving assistants, also called *helpers* and *packers,* aid drivers in packing and preparing household items and loading and unloading the van. Following instructions from the driver, they wrap fragile items in paper or cardboard and pack them in boxes or barrels. Moving assistants roll up rugs and remove pictures from walls. They make sure that all containers are labeled and identify the owner and the contents of the container. The labels are useful in organizing the items on the truck during the loading and unloading processes and also help if any items are misplaced. Assistants may use dollies, hoists, and hand trucks when carrying furniture, boxes, and other items to and from the truck. They pad furniture with blankets and secure the items in the truck into a compact load. Using ropes and straps, they carefully fasten the load in place so items do not move around unexpectedly and become damaged during the transportation process. At the destination, moving assistants unload and unpack everything, working under the direction of the driver.

Depending on the size of the move, usually three to six household movers are involved in the loading and unloading process. Their specific responsibilities can vary with the quantity and type of goods that are being moved and whether it is a local or long-distance move. If the customer is moving only a short distance, usually the same household movers load the van, accompany the driver to the destination, and unload the van. On a long-distance move, the van driver and an assistant usually drive to the destination and are met there by a local team of movers who help unload and set up the furniture.

REQUIREMENTS

High School
Although there are no specific educational requirements for work as a mover, most employers prefer to hire high school graduates. Experience in driving a truck and loading and unloading heavy material is an advantage.

Household movers need good oral and written communications skills because they must be able to understand and fill out an inventory list and follow detailed instructions. Van drivers are required to keep records of the material they move and the miles they drive, so they must have legible handwriting and basic math skills. Auto mechanics, English, and applied mathematics are high school courses that will provide you with a good background if you plan to work as a household mover. Courses in physical education will also help you prepare for the physical aspects of the job.

Certification or Licensing

While it is not a requirement for employment, many individuals apply to become certified professional movers as a way of demonstrating their professional qualifications in packing and moving services. Certification is awarded to movers who have had at least six months of experience and have passed certain examinations given by the American Moving and Storage Association. (See contact information at the end of this article.)

Other Requirements

Movers must be physically fit in order to move heavy objects. They also need stamina because they usually are on their feet lifting and carrying objects for hours at a time or driving for long periods.

To handle moving vans efficiently, drivers need to have good coordination and the ability to judge distances accurately. They must also be able to judge the capacity of trucks to avoid overloading them. An appropriate driver's license, usually a commercial driving permit, is required. In addition, independent operators may need to get operating permission from the Federal Motor Carrier Safety Administration and the U.S. Department of Transportation to transport furniture and other goods across state lines.

In most cases, movers must be at least 21 years old in order to work on interstate moves. In fact, individual moving firms may require their employees to be over 25 for insurance purposes.

EXPLORING

Because summer is the prime moving season, you may be able to secure a summer job as a moving assistant without prior experience. Part-time work may be available at other times of the year as well. If a job with a moving company is unavailable, look for a job in the shipping and receiving department of a large store. This type of work can provide you with firsthand experience of responsibilities similar to those of household movers.

Discussing the moving occupation with someone in the business can also be very informative. You can obtain additional information on this career at the library or by contacting the organizations at the end of this article.

EMPLOYERS

Moving companies may be local, regional, or national employers. Some retail furniture and department stores hire movers to deliver furniture, televisions, appliances, and other large objects to pur-chasers. In addition to working on household moves, workers are sometimes hired on a temporary assignment basis to help move and set up businesses.

STARTING OUT

To find a job as a household mover, contact moving companies directly. You also can look for job openings through newspaper classified ads or the local offices of your state's employment service. Moving companies usually provide beginning moving assistants with detailed instructions on packing procedures and filling out inventory lists before they start work.

ADVANCEMENT

Experienced furniture movers may advance into various related jobs. Moving assistants may be promoted to van drivers. Movers may also become dispatchers, who work in the main office of the mov-ing company and stay in constant contact with moving crews out on assignments. Another possibility is becoming an estimator. An estimator calculates the cost involved in a proposed move and quotes a price to the prospective customer.

Workers who have seniority and proven abilities may be able to move into supervisory positions where they coordinate the activities of drivers and help plan and direct other company operations. Some movers with enough knowledge, experience, and finances might go into business for themselves.

EARNINGS

Most furniture movers are paid on an hourly basis. Their wages depend on which area of the country they live in, the size of the company they work for, and their skills and experience level. Entry-level workers who pack, load, and unload freight (but do not drive trucks or vans) might expect to earn from $12,500 to $20,000 yearly. Laborers and freight, stock, and material movers earned median annual salaries of $20,610 in 2005, according to the U.S. Department of Labor. Some might eventually be able to make more than $35,000 annually.

The American Moving and Storage Association reported the fol-lowing average hourly salary ranges for household movers in the early 2000s: local drivers, $9.30 to $19.00; linehaul drivers, $4.00 to $24.50; packers, $4.00 to $19.75; and helpers, $4.58 to $15.00.

Because of their increased responsibilities, drivers earn somewhat more than assistants. They may have an income of around $18,000 to $38,000, depending on their skill and experience. Many van drivers belong to the International Brotherhood of Teamsters. The wages and benefits for union members are determined by agreements between unions and employers.

Most full-time movers receive benefits such as health insurance plans and paid vacation days, although union workers may receive more substantial benefit packages than nonunion workers.

WORK ENVIRONMENT

Movers spend a considerable amount of time outdoors, loading and unloading their cargo. They may find themselves moving furniture in extreme heat, below-freezing cold, snow, or rain. The work itself is physical and fairly strenuous, requiring the lifting of heavy and bulky objects, like couches and pianos. Movers have to learn techniques for lifting that minimize the chance of muscle strains and other injuries. Household movers may also spend large amounts of time packing and unpacking small fragile items like glassware, which can become tedious.

In much of the country, the summer months are the busiest times for household movers. Although the standard workweek for full-time employees is about 40 hours, they may work longer during this busy period, receiving overtime pay for extra hours worked.

Van drivers commonly work at least 50 hours a week, often under tiring and stressful conditions. Federal regulations limit their hours to no more than 60 hours on duty in any seven-day period. Also, after drivers have driven for 10 hours, they must be off duty for at least eight hours before they can drive again.

Interstate household movers, including van drivers, spend a considerable amount of time away from home.

OUTLOOK

On average, people in the United States move about once every five to seven years. This pattern is likely to continue in the foreseeable future, suggesting that the overall demand for movers is going to stay strong; however, there may be periods when fewer movers are needed. During economic downturns, people may avoid spending money by postponing moves or by doing part or all of the moving themselves. Employment opportunities will probably be strongest in large metropolitan areas simply because there are more people in these locations.

FOR MORE INFORMATION

For information on careers and certification in the moving and storage industry, contact

American Moving and Storage Association
1611 Duke Street
Alexandria, VA 22314-3406
Tel: 703-683-7410
Email: info@moving.org
http://promover.timberlakepublishing.com or http://www.moving.org

For information on union membership and benefits, contact

International Brotherhood of Teamsters
25 Louisiana Avenue, NW
Washington, DC 20001-2130
Tel: 202-624-6800
http://www.teamster.org

Household Workers

OVERVIEW

The category of *household workers* includes a number of occupations, all of which are concerned with the home. Household workers may clean homes, plan and cook meals, do laundry, administer the household account books, care for children, and perform numerous other duties, such as gardening and household maintenance.

HISTORY

For centuries, the size of a person's household staff was a measure of wealth and status. Although this may be true today to some extent, demand for household help has also been spurred by the rise in the general standard of living for most Americans and the increasing role of women in the workforce. Even families of modest means can often afford to hire help for a few hours to assist with cleaning or a caretaker to do household and garden maintenance on occasion. In the past, household work in the United States was often considered the first work-step on the economic ladder for immigrant families. Now the sons and daughters of those immigrant workers run many of the agencies that operate household services businesses.

THE JOB

The nature of the tasks performed by household workers can best be described by function. The *general houseworker* or *dayworker* is hired by the hour and fulfills numerous duties ranging from cleaning and making beds to buying, cooking, and serving food. The *personal attendant* performs personal services for the employer, such as mending, washing, and pressing garments; helping the employer dress; and keeping private quarters clean and tidy. *Caretakers* and *yard workers* do heavy housework and general home maintenance. They wash windows, wax floors, maintain heating and cooling systems, do odd jobs, and occasionally mow lawns or work in the garden.

Most households in the country can only afford to hire general houseworkers to work part time. These workers dust and polish furniture; sweep, mop, and wax floors; vacuum; and clean ovens, refrigerators, and bathrooms. They also wash dishes, polish silver, and take care of the laundry. Other duties may include looking after a child or an elderly family member, feeding and walking pets, calling and waiting for repair workers, and performing various errands. Houseworkers may have a regular set of duties, or they may be given different responsibilities each time they are engaged.

In larger, wealthier households, housekeepers usually have more responsibility and less supervision. At the pinnacle is the *home housekeeper,* who manages a household with a large staff of full-time workers. The home housekeeper directs the staff's activities, orders food and cleaning supplies, keeps a record of household expenses, and may even hire and fire workers.

The *domestic laundry worker, launderer,* or *presser* is usually restricted to the functions of maintaining clothes. The *cook* has broader responsibilities. The cook plans menus or works with the home housekeeper or family to plan special diets, prepares the food, serves meals, and performs such duties as making preserves and fancy pastries.

Child-care workers are responsible for the overall welfare of children in a household. They may wake them in the morning, put them to bed at night, and also bathe, dress, and feed them. They supervise the children's play and in-home educational activities and discipline them, if necessary. They may also take them to the doctor or other appointments.

Nannies usually care for children from birth to their preteen years. In addition to some general housekeeping duties, nannies oversee the children's early health, nutrition, and education, among other tasks.

Governesses assist in the general upbringing of children, from helping them with schoolwork, to teaching them a foreign language or other special skill, to ensuring that they learn proper manners. They may also perform some regular housekeeping duties.

Companions are on more of a par with their employers; indeed, they often are of the same social background. Their prime responsibility is to act as an aid or friend to a person who is elderly, disabled, convalescent, or merely living alone. Companions may tend to their employer's personal needs, such as bathing, dressing, and dispensing medicine. They may also look after social and business affairs, read to their employers, write letters for them, and perhaps most important, provide them with company.

Although women predominate in private household work, men also work in this field. A *valet* performs personal services for a male employer, such as caring for clothing, mixing and serving drinks, and running errands. The *butler,* like the home housekeeper, may supervise other household workers, assigning and coordinating their work. He also receives and announces guests, answers the telephone, and serves drinks. He may assign these duties to a second butler. A butler who is in charge of a large household staff is often called a *majordomo.*

REQUIREMENTS

High School

To be hired as a full-time household worker, you should have a high school diploma or its equivalent. Classes you may find beneficial to take include English to increase your communication skills and ability to follow directions and family and consumer science or home economics classes. If you are interested in a certain area of work, take classes that will increase your skills in those areas. For example, someone interested in lawn care and property maintenance might take horticulture or biology classes to learn about plant life and shop classes to learn how to use various tools. Someone interested in child care might take classes concentrating on child development and health. No matter what your area of interest, however, basic math classes will be useful. If your goal is to rise to a position such as home housekeeper or to own a cleaning business, you should also take accounting and business classes to help you prepare for the bookkeeping and other business aspects of the work.

Postsecondary Training

There are a number of schools across the country that offer specific training for positions such as butler, household manager, and nanny. For many jobs you will not need this additional training. However, those wishing to work in households employing a large staff or those wishing to advance their skills to increase employment possibilities may want to consider this option. Although these training programs can be expensive—some cost several thousand dollars—they typically provide job placement services to graduates.

Certification or Licensing

Those who graduate from postsecondary training programs may receive certification from their program. Like the training programs themselves, these certifications are voluntary. Certifications are also available from professional associations.

Other Requirements

A good personal appearance and demeanor are very important to a person who wishes to do household work. Because of the close contact between household workers and the members of the household, employers generally look for agreeable, discreet, and trustworthy individuals who have a neat, clean appearance and who are in good health. Much of the work done—whether out in the yard or in the house—involves a great deal of physical labor. Activities can include carrying, lifting, climbing, or standing for long periods of time. Anyone wanting to do this work, therefore, should be in good physical condition and have plenty of stamina.

EXPLORING

Those who enjoy housework and home repairs are likely to be successful household workers. One way to explore your interest in and enjoyment of this work is to get a part-time or summer job in this area. Although you may not immediately find employment in a private household, hotels and resorts frequently have positions available in cleaning, laundry, or even child care. During the summer, you may find business mowing people's lawns or caring for homes while owners are away on vacation. Another possibility is to do miscellaneous household and repair work for elderly people in your community who may want help with such tasks. Churches, synagogues, other religious organizations, or local employment offices may provide information on people looking for such help. Housekeeping, laundry, and kitchen opportunities may also be available on a summer or part-time basis at local nursing homes or hospitals. Volunteer opportunities also exist for those interested in being companions to persons needing personal assistance.

EMPLOYERS

Employers for household services can range from single apartment dwellers to homeowners with or without children to older persons looking for assistance or companionship. Some corporate apartment leasing companies may also hire household workers to clean and maintain their corporate housing units. Hotels, hospitals, and nursing homes also hire household workers for cleaning and repair duties. Most jobs are found in large cities and wealthy suburbs.

STARTING OUT

Most household workers find work through word-of-mouth. Friends or relatives may suggest homeowners who are looking for workers, while current and previous employers may often tell their friends about reliable household workers. Information about job opportunities is also available from local private employment agencies and state employment service offices.

Many self-employed household workers find jobs through newspaper ads. The Yellow Pages is a good source for companies that arrange housecleaning services. These companies will usually ask for previous experience and personal references. Direct contact with apartment complexes, hotels, and motels may also be a good way to get started in the household worker profession.

Training programs may offer job placement services to graduates of their programs.

ADVANCEMENT

Other than a wage increase, advancement is generally not available in households with only one or two workers. Top positions, such as butlers and housekeepers, usually require some specialized training. In addition, the turnover rate for these jobs is low, as is the number of households that can afford to offer such positions.

To advance, household workers can seek out new employers that pay more or require more skilled services. Workers may also move to similar jobs in hotels, hospitals, and restaurants, where the pay and fringe benefits are usually better and the work may be steadier.

Persons interested in further advancement may want to look into the certification programs available and seek employment with larger hotels, corporate housing, or other firms that hire household workers.

EARNINGS

The wages earned by household workers vary according to the kind of work performed, the number of hours worked, household and staff size, experience, and local standards of pay. Earnings vary from around $10 or more an hour in a big city to less than the minimum wage in some rural areas, according to the U.S. Department of Labor. Dayworkers often get carfare and a free meal. Live-in domestics usually earn more than dayworkers and also get free room and board, but they often work longer hours.

The U.S. Department of Labor reports that private household cooks and chefs earned hourly salaries that ranged from $6.35 (or $13,210 annually) to $16.81 ($34,960 annually) in 2005. According to the United States Personal Chef Association, personal chefs can earn from $35,000 to $50,000 a year. Child-care workers earned from $6.03 to $12.59 per hour (or approximately $12,540 to $26,190 per year for full-time work) in 2005, according to the U.S. Department of Labor. Experienced workers employed in large metropolitan areas by wealthy families, however, can earn from $40,000 to $60,000 per year. Those with experience and training may earn even more than these amounts. According to the U.S. Department of Labor, personal and home care aides earned from $6.00 to $11.04 an hour in 2005 (or approximately $12,480 to $22,970 annually for full-time work), with a median of $8.34 (or $17,340 annually for full-time work). Maids and housekeeping cleaners earned salaries that ranged from $12,820 to more than $25,700 in 2005.

According to the Starkey International Institute for Household Management, graduates of the Starkey training program who work as household managers earn from $40,000 to $150,000. Personal assistants earn from $80,000 to $100,000 and housing is provided. Salaries for household cooks are $30,000 to $45,000, and for household chefs, $40,000 to $55,000. Caretaker salaries range from an exchange of room and board for part-time duties to $40,000 per year, depending upon the size of the home and property. There are a limited number of employers at this elite level, of course, and such high-paying positions are rare.

Most household workers work part time, or less than 35 hours per week. Because of this, most household workers do not receive fringe benefits, such as health insurance, retirement plans, or paid vacation time.

WORK ENVIRONMENT

The work environment for household workers varies according to the duties performed. Some job responsibilities are done indoors and others, such as gardening and household repairs, may have to be performed outdoors.

Almost all household employees spend their working hours at the family residence; however, laundry workers may work in their own homes. Few household workers actually live with their employers for any period of time. Those who do usually enjoy a private room and a bath of their own.

Dayworkers often acquire several clients for whom they do cleaning and other chores on a part-time basis at specific intervals. Duties are negotiated with each employer, sometimes on a day-to-day basis. Even though modern washing and cleaning equipment and materials have helped considerably, housework can involve hard, dirty labor, especially for dayworkers who usually are given the heavier tasks to do. Some added demand for dayworkers picks up during the holiday season, but work tends to fall off for them and other household workers during the summer vacation months.

OUTLOOK

For many years, the demand for household help has outpaced the supply of workers willing to take domestic jobs. This imbalance is expected to persist and possibly worsen through 2014, according to the U.S. Department of Labor. Demand for household workers is expected to grow, as more families require both parents to work outside of the home and need help running their households. Demand for companions and personal attendants is also expected to rise due to the projected rapid growth of the elderly population. Worker supply is expected to remain low, however, because the work is physically demanding and usually offers low pay, no fringe benefits, and limited advancement potential. In addition, some people feel that this work carries with it a low social status. The general economic conditions also affect employment of household workers. During times of recession, household workers will find fewer employment opportunities.

While the field itself is not expected to grow, many jobs will be available for those interested in these occupations.

FOR MORE INFORMATION

For information on training, accredited programs, and a career as a nanny, contact
American Council of Nanny Schools
Thirty South Franklin Street
Chagrin Falls, OH 44022-3213
Tel: 800-733-1984
Email: administration@nanny-governess.com
http://www.americancouncilofnannyschools.com

The APCI holds seminars, offers a self-study course, and maintains an informative Web site with a personal chef message board.
American Personal Chef Institute (APCI)
4572 Delaware Street
San Diego, CA 92116-1005
Tel: 800-644-8389
Email: contact@personalchef.com
http://www.personalchef.com

For information on education opportunities for household managers, administrative household managers, personal assistants, and estate housekeepers, contact
International Institute of Household Management and Staffing
2000 Carriage Road
Powell, OH 43065-8688
Tel: 740-881-3358
http://www.worldclassservice.net

Professional Domestic Services & Institute
2000 Carriage Road
Powell, OH 43065-8688
Tel: 740-881-3358
http://www.professionaldomestics.com

Starkey International
1350 Logan Street
Denver, CO 80203-2309
Tel: 800-888-4904
Email: admissions@starkeyintl.com
http://www.starkeyintl.com

The USPCA offers training courses, certification, and mentorship.
United States Personal Chef Association (USPCA)
481 Rio Rancho Boulevard, NE
Rio Rancho, NM 87124-1421
Tel: 800-995-2138
http://www.uspca.com

Lawn and Gardening Service Owners

OVERVIEW

Lawn and gardening service owners maintain the lawns of residential and commercial properties. They cut grass and shrubbery, clean yards, and treat grass with fertilizer and insecticides. They may also landscape, which involves the arrangement of lawns, trees, and bushes. There are about 1.5 million people employed in the grounds maintenance industry. Approximately one out of every seven landscapers, groundskeepers, and nursery workers is self-employed.

HISTORY

If you've ever visited or seen photographs of the Taj Mahal in India or Versailles in France, then you've seen some elaborate examples of the lawns and gardens of the world. For as long as people have built grand palaces, they have designed lawns and gardens to surround them. Private, irrigated gardens of ancient Egypt and Persia were regarded as paradise with their thick, green vegetation and cool shade. In the 16th century, Italians kept gardens that wound about fountains, columns, and steps. The English developed the "cottage-style" gardens to adhere to the natural surroundings. Early American gardens, such as those surrounding Monticello in Virginia, were inspired by this English style.

The English also inspired the Georgian style of house design in the 18th century that caught on across Europe and America. Rows of houses down city blocks were designed as units, their yards hidden

QUICK FACTS

School Subjects
Agriculture
Technical/shop

Personal Skills
Following instructions
Mechanical/manipulative

Work Environment
Primarily outdoors
Primarily multiple locations

Minimum Education Level
High school diploma

Salary Range
$20,000 to $50,000 to $100,000+

Certification or Licensing
Required by certain states

Outlook
Faster than the average

DOT
408

GOE
03.04.04

NOC
N/A

O*NET-SOC
37-1012.00, 37-1012.01

behind the houses and away from the streets. Lawn care as a business blossomed with the growth of population and home ownership between the Civil War and World War I. The sport of golf also became popular among the rich at this time, spurring further development of lawn care products and machinery. Since World War II, many people now hire lawn maintenance professionals to keep up and improve the look of their personal lawns and gardens.

THE JOB

Lawn and gardening businesses may choose to offer only a few services, such as lawn mowing and hedge clipping. But some businesses offer a large number of services, from simple cleaning to the actual design of the yard. Some lawn services specialize in organic lawn care. They rely on natural fertilizers and applications to control insects and lawn diseases instead of applying toxic chemicals to treat lawns.

When working for private homeowners, lawn and gardening services do yard work once or twice a week for each client. They arrive at the residence with equipment, such as a push or riding mower, an aerator, and a blower vac. Workers cut the grass and "weed eat," trimming the weeds at the edges of the houses and fences. They also apply fertilizer and insecticide to the lawn to keep the grass healthy and use an aerator to run over the yard to make holes in the topsoil and allow more airflow.

Lawn and gardening service owners participate in all aspects of the business, including the labor. They plant grass seed in areas where there is little growth, and use blowers to blow leaves and other debris from the yard, sidewalks, and driveway. Lawn services are often called in after storms and other natural disasters to clean up and repair lawns.

"There are a lot of little services you can throw in to keep yourself busy," says Sam Morgan, who operates a lawn care service in Dallas, Texas. He does general lawn maintenance for residential yards and some rental properties. "Having some rental property can be good," he says. "It's year-round work. But it can also be dirty work; you have to pick up a lot of trash."

In addition to mowing yards and weed eating, he assists with planting flower beds, cleaning house gutters, and some light tree work. Tree care involves the pruning and trimming of branches. Lawn and gardening services may need to remove dead or unwanted trees before planting new ones. They may also offer landscaping services, offering advice on arranging the lawn. Service owners assist in positioning trees, bushes, fountains, flower beds, and lighting. They may also put up wood or metal fencing, and install sprinkler systems.

"I started the business on a shoestring," Morgan says. "But I learned early that you have to have good equipment." He now owns a commercial mower that can handle 200 yards a week.

Lawn and gardening service owners have responsibilities other than just lawn and garden care. As owners, they are responsible for the business end of the service. In order to stay in business, owners must balance the budget, collect on accounts, repair or replace equipment when necessary, order supplies, and, depending on the size of the business, hire and manage other employees.

In addition to working on the demanding yard work, Morgan spends much of his time attending to business details, such as keeping tax records, making phone calls, and preparing estimates and bills.

REQUIREMENTS

High School
Take agriculture, shop, and other courses that will help you gain familiarity with the machinery, fertilizers, and chemicals used in lawn maintenance. Agriculture courses will also teach you about different grasses and plants, and how to care for them. Joining associations such as the National FFA Organization (formerly the Future Farmers of America) and 4-H can give you additional experience with horticulture. Business and accounting courses are also useful to learn about record keeping, budgeting, and finances.

Postsecondary Training
After high school, you can learn about lawn maintenance while on the job, either by assisting someone with an established lawn care business, or by taking on a few residential customers yourself. Though a college degree is not necessary, lawn and gardening service owners benefit from advanced courses such as small business management and finance to help run their business.

Certification or Licensing
Certification is not required, but many lawn and garden service owners choose to earn professional certifications from the Professional Landcare Network. The network offers the following certification designations: certified landscape professional, certified landscape technician-interior, certified landscape technician-exterior, certified

turfgrass professional, certified turfgrass professional-cool season lawns, and certified ornamental landscape professional. Depending on the certification, applicants must pass a multiple-choice examination or a hands-on field test.

Most states require lawn care professionals who apply pesticides to be licensed. This usually involves passing a written examination on the safe use and disposal of toxic chemicals.

Other Requirements

As entrepreneurs, lawn and gardening service owners need to have people skills and be self-motivated to successfully promote their own business and attract clients.

"I'm a good salesman," Sam Morgan says. He also emphasizes the need to be committed to doing a quality job for every customer. Service owners should have an eye for detail to notice all the areas where lawns need work. They must also be in fairly good health to withstand the hard labor that the job calls for, often during the heat of the summer.

EXPLORING

If you've made some extra money mowing lawns for your neighbors, then you're already familiar with many of the aspects of a lawn care service. Walking behind a power mower during the hottest days of the year may make you miserable, but early experience in keeping your next-door neighbor's lawn looking nice is a great opportunity for self-employment. Other sources for potential clients are private homeowners, apartment complex communities, golf courses, and parks. Look into volunteer and part-time work with botanical gardens, greenhouses, and park and recreation crews.

Opportunities to learn how to care for a lawn and garden are no farther than your own backyard. Experiment with planting and maintaining different varieties of flowers, shrubs, or trees. Chances are, you'll gain valuable experience and your parents will thank you!

In addition to getting dirt under your fingernails, you can also explore the lawn and garden services by reading magazines and books on lawn and garden care. Cable television stations, such as Home and Garden Television (HGTV), feature programming about gardening.

Every summer, many high school students find reliable work mowing lawns. But many of these students tire of the work early in the summer. Be persistent in seeking out work all summer long. You should also be committed to doing good work; you'll have stiff competition from professional lawn care businesses that offer more services, own commercial machinery, and have extensive knowledge of fertilizers and pesticides. Some lawn care companies also hire students for summer work.

EMPLOYERS

Lawn and gardening service owners work primarily for private homeowners, though they may also contract work with commercial properties. Condos, hotels, apartment complexes, golf courses, sports fields, and parks all require regular lawn service.

Owners who choose to build their own business face challenges such as covering the costs of start up and establishing a client base. To defray these costs and risks, many choose to purchase and operate an existing business. There are a number of franchise opportunities in lawn care that, for a fee, will assist you in promoting your business and building a clientele. Emerald Green Lawn Care, Liqui-Green Lawn Care, and Lawn Doctor are just a few. NaturaLawn of America is a franchise that provides organic-based lawn care.

STARTING OUT

Most lawn and gardening service owners start out working for established services and work their way into positions of management or higher responsibility. A typical entry-level job is that of the landscape service technician. After a few years on the job, promising technicians may be promoted to supervisor positions such as regional or branch managers. According to the Professional Landcare Network, "once a supervisory position is reached, leadership is the key to success." Workers who are organized, show strong leadership, and can make decisions quickly and wisely will have the best chances for promotion and may choose to start up their own business.

Not all service owners follow this route, though. Sam Morgan's lawn service was not his first venture into entrepreneurship; he had once owned a number of dry cleaners. After selling the dry cleaners, he went to work for a chemical company. When the company downsized, Morgan was faced with finding a new job. He decided to turn to lawn care.

"I just went to Sears and bought a mower," he says. Since then, he's been able to invest in commercial machinery that can better handle the demands of the work, and he's found a number of ways to increase business. "I bill once a month," he says. "I get more business that way." He's also expanding his service to include some light landscaping, such as shrub work and planting small trees.

Depending on the business, start-up costs can vary. To purchase commercial quality equipment, the initial investment can be between

$3,000 and $4,000. To buy into a franchise, however, will cost thousands of dollars more.

ADVANCEMENT

Once lawn and gardening service owners establish their own businesses, advancement can come in the form of expanded services. Some lawn professionals offer equipment and supply sales. With extended services, owners can reach out to a larger body of clients, securing larger contracts with golf courses, cities and local communities, and sports teams.

Sam Morgan currently has one employee, but he hopes for his business to grow more, allowing him to hire others. "I don't want to be doing so much of the physical work," he says.

With additional education, owners can also advance into other areas of lawn care and become contractors or landscape architects.

EARNINGS

Earnings in lawn care depend on a number of factors, such as geographic location, the size of the business, and the level of experience. Lawn care services generally make more money in areas of the country that have mild winters, offering more months of lawn growth and, as a result, requiring more care. The size of the client base also greatly affects earnings. A lawn care professional with a small clientele may make less than $20,000 a year, while the owner of a franchise lawn care company with a number of contracts and a large staff can make over $100,000.

According to 2005 data from the U.S. Department of Labor, first-line supervisors/managers of landscaping, lawn service, and groundskeeping workers made an average of $17.46 an hour (or $36,320 annually). Salaries ranged from less than $23,240 to $58,470 or more annually. The Professional Landcare Network offers the following summary of earnings potential for management positions: first-level supervisors, $35,000; branch managers, $50,000 or more; regional managers, $60,000s; and successful owners, $100,000 or more.

WORK ENVIRONMENT

To many, working on a lawn or garden is relaxing, and the opportunity to work outdoors during pleasant days of spring and summer is enjoyable. The work can also be exhausting and strenuous, though. Lawn and gardening service owners fully involved in the labor of the business may have to lift heavy equipment from trucks, climb trees, and do a lot of walking, kneeling, and bending on the job. Depending on the nature of the business, service owners may have to exercise caution when handling harmful chemicals used in pesticides. In addition, they have to deal with a loud work environment because machinery such as lawn mowers, weed eaters, and blow vacs can be very noisy.

One benefit of owning a business is the ability to create a flexible work schedule. "Most likely," Sam Morgan says, "during the spring and summer, you can make plenty of money. There's plenty of work to be done." But some of that work may be in the hottest days of the summer, or on rainy days. With your own service, you can arrange to work regular weekday hours, or you can schedule weekends.

OUTLOOK

The benefits of a nice lawn aren't just aesthetic; a well-kept lawn can increase property value and provide a safe place for children to play. According to a 2004 survey conducted by the Associated Landscape Contractors of America, consumers spent $37.9 billion on professional landscape and lawn services in 2003, marking growth of 31 percent from the previous year.

This spending promises a good future for lawn care services. The sale of lawn care products is expected to grow as more houses are built and more people recognize the importance of quality lawn care. The Environmental Protection Agency promotes the environmental benefits of a healthy lawn, emphasizing that healthy grass is not only attractive, but controls dust and pollens, provides oxygen, and improves the quality of groundwater. More people now recognize that a nice lawn can increase home value by as much as 20 percent, according to studies.

Technological developments will also aid the industry. With better, more economical equipment, lawn care professionals can do more specialized work in less time, allowing them to keep their service fees low.

FOR MORE INFORMATION

For general information about franchising, specific franchise opportunities, and the publication Franchising World Magazine, *contact the IFA.*

International Franchise Association (IFA)
1501 K Street, NW, Suite 350
Washington, DC 20005-1412
Tel: 202-628-8000

Email: ifa@franchise.org
http://www.franchise.org

To further explore the agriculture industry and for information on student chapters, contact
National FFA Organization
6060 FFA Drive
PO Box 68960
Indianapolis, IN 46268-0960
Tel: 317-802-6060
http://www.ffa.org

For information on certification, careers, internships, and student membership, contact
Professional Landcare Network
950 Herndon Parkway, Suite 450
Herndon, VA 20170-5528
Tel: 800-395-2522
http://www.landcarenetwork.org/cms/home.html

═══ INTERVIEW ═══

Guillermo Ramirez has owned a landscaping service for 31 years. He discussed his career with the editors of Careers in Focus: Personal Services.

Q. Please briefly describe your job responsibilities as a landscaping service owner.

A. The main goal is to keep the customer happy. I do this by attending to all of the physical needs of their lawn (cutting, trimming, edging, weeding, etc.) on a regular basis to keep it looking its best. My secondary job responsibilities consist of performing routine maintenance on my equipment.

Q. What are the most important qualities for landscape service owners?

A. You need to be detail oriented and a hard worker. This field can be very physical with some days requiring long hours. You also need to be a people person. You will deal with customers, and they are your livelihood, so you have to be able to interact with them and attend to their specific needs and see things from their point of view. You also need to be easygoing. This field depends on something that you can't control—the weather—so you need a flexible and easygoing attitude when Mother Nature isn't cooperative.

Q. What are some of the pros and cons of your job?

A. Pros: You are your own boss, so there's some flexibility to your schedule and when you choose to take on jobs. The season is only eight months long so you have four months of down time where you can do whatever you like—such as travel.

Cons: Because the job depends on the weather, things sometimes do not work out as planned and schedules need to be adjusted.

Q. What advice would you give to young people who are interested in entering this field?

A. Go for it! As long as you like working with people, this field is a rewarding one to enter.

Locksmiths

QUICK FACTS

School Subjects
Mathematics
Technical/shop

Personal Skills
Mechanical/manipulative
Technical/scientific

Work Environment
Indoors and outdoors
Primarily multiple locations

Minimum Education Level
Some postsecondary training

Salary Range
$10,712 to $30,880 to
$50,390+

Certification or Licensing
Voluntary (certification)
Required by certain states
(licensing)

Outlook
About as fast as the average

DOT
709

GOE
05.03.01

NOC
7383

O*NET-SOC
49-9094.00

OVERVIEW

Locksmiths, or lock experts, are responsible for all aspects of installing and servicing locking devices, such as door and window locks for buildings, door and ignition locks for automobiles, locks on such objects as combination safes and desks, and electronic access control devices. Locksmiths are often considered to be artisans or craftspeople who combine ingenuity with mechanical aptitude. There are approximately 28,000 locksmiths employed in the United States.

HISTORY

Guarding and protecting families and possessions is an ancient practice that has led throughout the centuries to widespread use of various types of locking devices. Locks have been, and still are, used to secure residences, commercial buildings, and other items, such as automobiles and safe deposit boxes. The oldest known lock and key device, which dates to about 4,000 years ago and is quite large, was found in the ruins of the Khorsabad palace near the biblical city of Nineveh. That lock was of the wooden pin-tumbler type, a form that was widely used in Egypt and also found in Japan, Norway, and the Faeroe Islands (and is still being used in parts of the Near East today). The modern Yale cylinder lock is actually based on this Egyptian pin-tumbler mechanism.

Roman locksmiths introduced metal locks (made primarily of iron and bronze), padlocks, and warded locks, which are made with varied projections around the keyhole. They also designed keys fashioned as rings so they could be carried easily, supposedly because togas had no pockets. Another important Roman contribution was the craft of making small locks to be used with tiny keys. Elaborate and intricate decorative surface designs introduced by craftspeople in Germany and France during the Middle Ages transformed locks into works of art; however, these locks showed little improvement in safety and security.

Special machines allow locksmiths to create and duplicate keys for any lock. The history of the industry includes a list of locksmiths who contributed to design developments. In 1778, the Englishman Robert Barron patented a lever lock with double-acting tumblers. Just 40 years later, his fellow countryman, Jeremiah Chubb, improved on the reliability of the lever lock by incorporating a detector in its mechanism. Meanwhile, in 1784, Joseph Bramah, also from England, had introduced his innovative Bramah lock and key, which was to remain "unpickable" for more than 50 years. In 1851, Robert Newell of New York exhibited his Parautoptic lock, which reputedly remains unpicked to this day.

In 1848, Linus Yale, of the United States, patented a pin-tumbler lock, from which his son, Linus Jr., devised the Yale cylinder lock during the 1860s. James Sargent of Rochester, New York, adapted an earlier Scots patent in 1873 for a lock that incorporated a clock, allowing vaults and safes to be opened only at preset times. Other lock experts experimented with the letter-lock until the keyless combination device was perfected.

Since the 1800s, many other types of locks have been devised for specific purposes. The most reputable and the most commonly used of today's nonelectronic locks, however, are direct descendants of the original Yale cylinder, the Bramah, and combination devices.

The advent of new technology in the middle to late 20th century has led to increased and widespread use of electronic-access control devices. Such security equipment is based on fundamental electronic wiring and utilizes any of a variety of mechanisms, such as plastic credit card-shaped "keys" with magnetic code strips or electronic button-coded doorknobs. Electronic access control devices have replaced manually operated locks in many circumstances, from large building complexes to automobile doors. New lock technology has resulted from the demands by security-conscious citizenry for complicated, sophisticated locks. Because such devices require skilled and knowledgeable care, some say that locksmiths have never had it so good.

THE JOB

The aspects of the locksmith profession differ, depending on whether one works for one's own business, in a shop for a master locksmith, or as an in-house lock expert for a large establishment, such as an apartment complex or a high-rise office building. However, the essential nature of the work for all locksmiths can be described in general terms. Basically, they sell, service, and install locks, spending part of their working time in locksmith shops and part of it at the sites they are servicing. Locksmiths install locks in homes, offices, factories, and many other types of establishments. In addition to maintaining the working mechanics of lock devices, locksmiths usually perform functions that include metalworking, carpentry, and electronics.

The basic equipment used by the locksmith includes a workbench, various tools, a key machine, and supplies. Tools may include broken key extractors, drills, files, key blanks, springs, C-clamps, circular hole cutters, hammers, and screwdrivers.

While at the shop, locksmiths work on such portable items as padlocks and luggage locks, as well as on an endless number of keys. When they need to do work at a customer's site, they usually drive to the site in a work van that carries an assortment of the locksmith's most common equipment and supplies. When on site, they perform whatever function is needed for each specific job, be it opening locks whose keys have been lost, preparing master-key systems for such places as hotels and apartment complexes, removing old locks and installing modern devices, or rewiring electronic access control devices. Because locks are commonly found on doors and other building structures, lock experts often put their carpentry skills to use when doors have to be fitted for locks. And because locking devices are increasingly made with electronic parts, locksmiths must use their knowledge and skill to work with electronic door openers, electromagnetic locks, and electrical keyless locks.

Lock experts may spend part of their working day providing service to those who have locked themselves out of their houses, places of work, or vehicles. When keys are locked inside, locksmiths must pick the lock. If keys are lost, new ones often must be made. Locksmiths often repair locks by taking them apart to examine, clean, file, and adjust the cylinders and tumblers. Combination locks present a special task for locksmiths; they must be able to open a safe, for example, if its combination lock does not work smoothly. Manipulating combination locks requires expert, precise skills that are honed by much practice. The technique requires that the locksmith listen for vibrations and for the interior mechanism to indicate a change in direction while the dial is carefully rotated; this is repeated until the mechanism has been accurately turned. If it isn't possible to open the lock through these methods, the device may be drilled.

Locksmiths work in any community large enough to need their services, but most jobs are available in large metropolitan areas. Some locksmiths work in shops for other professionals, and others work for large hardware or department stores. Also, many open their own businesses. Independent locksmiths must perform all the tasks needed to run any type of business, such as keeping books and tax records, preparing statements, ordering merchandise, and advertising. A locksmith's clients may include individual home or automobile owners as well as large organizations such as hospitals, housing developments, military bases, and federal agencies. Industrial complexes and huge factories may employ locksmiths to install and maintain complete security systems, and other establishments, such as school systems and hotels, employ locksmiths to regularly install or change locks. Many locksmiths are getting more involved in the security aspect of the profession and may be required to analyze security needs and propose, monitor, and maintain security systems for businesses and residences.

REQUIREMENTS

High School

No special educational requirements are needed to become a locksmith. Most employers prefer applicants who have graduated from high school. Helpful school classes include metal shop, mathematics, mechanical drawing, computers, and electronics, if available.

Postsecondary Training

There are locksmiths who have learned their skills from professionals in the business, but many workers learn the trade by either attending a community college or trade school or completing an accredited correspondence course. A number of trade schools in the United States follow a curriculum based on all practical aspects of the locksmith trade. They teach the correct application of the current range of security devices, including the theory and practice of electronic access control, as well as the servicing and repairing of mortise, cylindrical, and bit-key locks. Students learn to recognize keys by their manufacturer and practice cutting keys by hand as well as by machine. Some courses allow students to set up a sample master-key system for clients such as a business or apartment complex. In addition to these fundamentals, pupils also learn to use carpentry tools and jigs to install common locking devices. Finally, they learn about automobile lock systems (how to enter locked automobiles in emergencies and how to remove, service, and repair ignition locks) and combination locks (how to service interchangeable core cylinders and manipulate combinations). The objective of such training is to teach the prospective locksmith all of the basic responsibilities. After completing a training course, the graduate should be able to meet customer demand and standards of the trade with minimum supervision.

Many persons interested in a locksmith career learn the trade by taking correspondence courses, which include instructions, assignments, tools, and model locks and keys. Lessons may be supplemented with supervised on-the-job training with a consenting master locksmith.

Certification or Licensing

Many cities and states require that locksmiths be licensed and bonded. In some areas, locksmiths may have to be fingerprinted and pay a fee to be licensed.

Area and state locksmith associations may require that their members be certified. The Associated Locksmiths of America (ALA) offers the following certification designations: registered locksmith, certified registered locksmith, certified professional locksmith, and, the highest level, certified master locksmith. The ALA also offers the following certification designations to locksmiths who specialize in installing and servicing locks and other security devices on safes and vaults: certified professional safetech and certified master safetech. Contact the ALA for more information.

Other Requirements

Locksmiths must be able to plan and schedule jobs and to use the right tools, techniques, and materials for each. Good vision and hearing are necessary for working with combination locks, and eye-hand coordination is essential when working with tiny locks and their intricate interiors. A good locksmith should have both a delicate touch and an understanding of the nature of mechanical devices.

Each lost key, broken lock, and security problem will present a unique challenge that the locksmith must be prepared to remedy on the spot. Locksmiths, therefore, must be able to think well on their feet. Locksmiths also have a responsibility to be reliable, accurate, and, most important, honest, since their work involves the security of persons and valuables. Customers must be able to count on the locksmith's skill, dependability, and integrity. In addition, locksmiths must be aware of laws that apply to elements of their jobs, such as restrictions on duplicating master keys, making safe deposit box keys, and opening automobiles whose keys are not available. It is suggested that the locksmith-to-be consult with a lawyer to discuss the legal responsibilities of the trade.

EXPLORING

High school machine shop classes will provide you with a degree of experience in using a variety of hand tools, some of which may be used in the trade. If you are interested in learning specifically about types of locks and how to work with them, read *The Complete Book of Locks and Locksmithing* (New York: McGraw-Hill Professional, 2005), or other books about the trade that may be available at local libraries or bookstores.

It is a good idea to contact organizations that are involved with the locksmithing trade. You might request information from the Associated Locksmiths of America, whose objective is to educate and provide current information to those involved in the physical security industry. Another method of finding out more about the career is to talk with someone already employed as a locksmith.

EMPLOYERS

Approximately 28,000 locksmiths are employed in the United States. The largest demand for locksmiths is in larger metropolitan areas. Many locksmiths are hired by locksmith shops or large hardware or department stores. Numerous large factories, resorts, hotels and industrial facilities hire locksmiths to install and change their locks and to maintain their security systems. Many locksmiths open their own businesses and provide services to home or automobile owners, as well as to hospitals, hotels, motels, businesses, government facilities, and housing developments.

Learn More About It

Friend, Mick. *The Encyclopaedia For Locksmiths*. Gamlingay, U.K.: Authors Online, 2004.
Hampton, Steve. *Modern High-Security Locks: How To Open Them*. Boulder, Colo.: Paladin Press, 2002.
Kostman, Joel. *Keys to the City: Tales of a New York City Locksmith*. New York: Penguin Books, 1999.
Phillips, Bill. *The Complete Book of Locks and Locksmithing* 6th ed. New York: McGraw-Hill Professional, 2005.

The increased use of security systems in businesses and residences offers many additional employment options for locksmiths. These jobs may require additional training and skills, however.

STARTING OUT

Since locksmithing is a vocation that requires skill and experience, it is unlikely that the untrained job seeker will be able to begin immediately in the capacity of locksmith. Beginners might consider contacting local shops to inquire about apprenticeships. In some cases, skilled locksmiths may be willing to teach their trade to a promising worker in exchange for low-cost labor. Another method is to check with state employment offices for business and industry listings of job openings for locksmiths. Some locksmith trade organizations may post job openings or apprenticeships.

Students enrolled in a trade school can obtain career counseling and job placement assistance. Trade school graduates should be qualified to begin work in established locksmith shops doing basic work both in the shop and on the road; others become in-house locksmiths for businesses and other establishments.

ADVANCEMENT

Most locksmiths regard their work as a lifetime profession. They stay abreast of new developments in the field so that they can increase both their skills and earnings. As they gain experience, industrial locksmiths may advance from apprentices to journeymen to master locksmiths, to any of several kinds of supervisory or managerial positions.

After having worked in the field for a number of years, many lock experts decide to establish their own shops and businesses. In doing so, they tend to build working relationships with a list of clients and, in effect, can grow their business at their own flexible rate. Self-employed locksmiths are responsible for all the tasks that are required to run a business, such as planning, organizing, bookkeeping, and marketing.

Another advancement opportunity lies in becoming a specialist in any of a number of niches. Some locksmiths work exclusively with combination locks, for example, or become experts in automobile devices. One of the most promising recent specialty growth areas is that of electronic security. Such safety devices and systems are becoming standard equipment for large establishments such as banks, hotels, and many industries, as well as residences and autos, and their popularity is creating a need for skilled locksmiths to install and service them.

EARNINGS

Locksmithing can be a lucrative occupation, depending upon the geographic region of the country and the type of work done. Geographically, wages for locksmiths tend to follow the pattern of general earnings of all occupations; that is, workers on the East Coast tend to earn the most and those in the South and Southwest the least.

Entry-level locksmiths with no experience generally start out with wages between minimum wage and $7 an hour, although in some areas wages may be higher. Experienced locksmiths earned an average of $30,880 annually in 2005, according to the U.S. Department of Labor. Locksmiths with considerable experience and a large clientele can earn more than $50,390 annually. Locksmiths who specialize in high-security electronic systems may earn much more than that. Full-time employees can usually expect general fringe benefits.

Self-employed locksmiths may be small business operators who earn less than some salaried employees, or they may head larger operations and earn more than the average through contracts with numerous clients.

WORK ENVIRONMENT

Locksmiths who are self-employed often work up to 60 hours per week; apprentices and locksmiths working in industries and institutions, however, usually work standard 40-hour workweeks. Some locksmith businesses may offer after-hour services. These employers may require locksmiths to answer service calls at any time of the day or night, including weekends.

Locksmiths stand during much of their working time, but they also often need to crouch, bend, stoop, and kneel. Sometimes they are required to lift heavy gates, doors, and other objects when dealing with safes, strong rooms, or lock fittings.

Locksmith workshops are usually well lit, well heated, and well ventilated. Some shops, particularly mobile ones, however, may be crowded and small, requiring that workers move carefully around fixtures and stock. Some locksmiths work outdoors, installing or repairing protective or warning devices. Some workers who work at other sites may have to do considerable driving. Locksmiths may work alone or may be required at times to work with others at stores, banks, factories, schools, and other facilities. Physical injuries are not common, but minor ones can occur from soldering irons, welding equipment, electric shocks, flying bits from grinders, and sharp lock or key edges.

OUTLOOK

The U.S. Department of Labor predicts that employment for locksmiths will grow about as fast as the average for all occupations through 2014. Population growth and an expanding public awareness of the need for preventive measures against home, business, and auto burglary continue to create needs for security devices and their maintenance. Also, many individuals and firms are replacing older lock and alarm systems with the latest developments in computerized equipment. Consequently, opportunities will be best for those workers who are able to install and service electronic security systems.

The locksmith trade itself has remained stable, with few economic fluctuations, and locksmiths with an extensive knowledge of their trade are rarely unemployed.

FOR MORE INFORMATION

For information on schools and colleges that offer locksmith classes, contact

Accrediting Commission of Career Schools and Colleges of Technology
2101 Wilson Boulevard, Suite 302
Arlington, VA 22201-3062
Tel: 703-247-4212
Email: info@accsct.org
http://www.accsct.org

For information on locksmithing careers, certification, education, and scholarships, contact

Associated Locksmiths of America
3500 Easy Street
Dallas, TX 75247-6416
Tel: 800-532-2562
Email: education@aloa.org
http://www.aloa.org

For a list of accredited home-study programs in locksmithing, contact
Distance Education and Training Council
1601 18th Street, NW
Washington, DC 20009-2529
Tel: 202-234-5100
Email: detc@detc.org
http://www.detc.org

Nannies

QUICK FACTS

School Subjects
Family and consumer science
Psychology

Personal Skills
Communication/ideas
Helping/teaching

Work Environment
Primarily indoors
Primarily one location

Minimum Education Level
High school diploma

Salary Range
$20,800 to $24,960 to
$31,200

Certification or Licensing
Voluntary

Outlook
About as fast as the average

DOT
301

GOE
10.03.03

NOC
6474

O*NET-SOC
39-9011.00

OVERVIEW

Nannies, also known as *au pairs*, are caregivers who care for children in the parents' homes. The children usually range in age from infant to 11 years old. The nanny's responsibilities may include supervising the nursery, organizing play activities, taking the children to appointments or classes, and keeping the children's quarters clean and intact. They may be responsible for supervising the child for part of the day or the entire day.

In a large and growing percentage of American families, both parents hold full-time jobs and require full-time child care, which has resulted in increased employment opportunities for nannies. In many other families, parents are opting for part-time work or running businesses out of their homes. Although this allows the parents to be with their children more than if they worked a traditional job, the unpredictability of children's needs makes a nanny's help welcome. A growing segment of parents prefer that their children be cared for at home as opposed to taking them to day care or a babysitter. Thus, the nanny has become a viable and often satisfactory solution.

HISTORY

Nannies have been a staple of European staffs for hundreds of years, often epitomizing the upper-class British childhood. They have captured our imaginations and have been the basis for fictional characters ranging from Jane Eyre to Mary Poppins. In the United States, nannies or nursemaids have worked in the homes of the very wealthy for centuries. Only quite recently, however, has the role of the nanny entered the lives of the middle class.

Because of the steadily increasing demand for highly skilled, reliable, private child care, nannies have gained such popularity that schools have sprung up across the country to train and place them. The vast majority of nannies come from overseas, however. Young women and men from the West Indies, the Philippines, Ireland, South Central America, and other regions often emigrate to the United States to become nannies because of the poor economic conditions in their own countries. These nannies are often taken advantage of by the people for whom they work. They may be paid next to nothing, and be expected to be completely at the disposal of the family, even at a moment's notice, and they usually receive no health insurance or other benefits. Unfortunately, they put up with this sort of treatment mainly because they are afraid to lose the income, a large part of which they often send home to relatives in their native country.

With proper training and placement, however, nannies can find their jobs to be pleasant, satisfying experiences.

THE JOB

Nannies perform their child-care duties in the homes of the families that employ them. Unlike other kinds of household help, nannies are specifically concerned with the needs of the children in their charge. Nannies prepare the children's meals, making sure they are nutritious, appealing, and appetizing. They may do grocery shopping specifically for the children. Nannies may attend the children during their mealtimes and oversee their training in table manners and proper etiquette. They also clean up after the children's meals. If there is an infant in the family, a nanny will wash and sterilize bottles and feed the infant. It is not part of a nanny's regular duties to cook for the adult members of the household or do domestic chores outside of those required for the children.

Nannies are responsible for keeping order in the children's quarters. They may clean the bedrooms, nursery, and playrooms, ensuring beds are made with clean linens and sufficient blankets. Nannies may also wash and iron the children's clothing and do any necessary mending. They make sure that the clothing is neatly put away. With older children, the nanny may begin instructions in orderliness and neatness, teaching children how to organize their possessions.

Nannies bathe and dress the children and instill proper grooming skills. Children often seek the assistance of their nanny in getting ready for family parties or holidays. As the children get older, nannies help them learn how to dress themselves and take care of their appearance.

Nannies must possess an even and generous temperament when working with children. *(Jim Whitmer Photography)*

Not only are nannies responsible for the care and training of their charges, but they also act as companions and guardians. They plan games and learning activities for the children and supervise their play, encouraging fairness and good sportsmanship. They may be responsible for planning activities to commemorate holidays, special events, or birthdays. These activities may center on field trips, arts and crafts, or parties. Nannies may travel with families on trips and vacations, or they may take the children on short excursions without their families. Nannies must be detail oriented when it comes to the children entrusted to their care. They keep records of illnesses, allergies, and injuries. They also note learning skills and related progress as well as personal achievements, such as abilities in games or arts and crafts. Later, they relate these events and achievements to the parents.

Nannies act as the parents' assistants by focusing closely on the children and fostering the behavior expected of them. They are responsible for carrying out the parents' directions for care and activities. By setting good examples and helping the children follow guidelines established by their parents, nannies encourage the development of happy and confident personalities.

REQUIREMENTS

High School

From an educational standpoint, nannies usually are required to have at least a high school diploma or equivalent (GED). Helpful high school classes include health, psychology, and home economics. English and communications classes are also useful, as they provide skills that will help in everyday dealings with the children and their parents. Nannies usually must also have a valid driver's license, since they may be asked to chauffeur the children to doctors' appointments or other outings.

Postsecondary Training

There are several schools that offer specialized nanny training, which usually lasts between 12 and 16 weeks. These programs are typically accredited by individual state agencies. Employers generally prefer applicants who have completed an accredited program. Graduates of accredited programs also can command higher salaries.

Two- and four-year programs are available at many colleges and include courses on early childhood education, child growth and development, and child care. College course work in nanny training may also focus on communication, family health, first aid, child psychology, and food and nutrition. Classes may include play and recreational games, arts and crafts, children's literature, and safety and health. Because nannies may be responsible for children of various ages, the course work focuses on each stage of childhood development and the particular needs of individual children. Special emphasis is given to the care of infants. Professional nanny schools may also give instruction on family management, personal appearance, and appropriate conduct.

Certification or Licensing

Nannies who have graduated from a nanny school that is accredited by the American Council of Nanny Schools can use the title certified professional nanny. Certification shows potential employers your commitment to the work as well as your level of training.

Other Requirements

Nannies must possess an even and generous temperament when working with children. They must be kind, affectionate, and genuinely interested in the child's well-being and development. Good physical condition, energy, and stamina are also necessary for success in this career. Nannies must be able to work well on their own initiative and have sound judgment to handle any small crises or emergencies that arise. They must know how to instill discipline and carry out the parents' expectations.

They should be loyal and committed to the children and respect the families for whom they work. In some cases, this is difficult, since nannies are often privy to negative elements of family life, which can include the emotional problems of parents and their neglect of their children. Nannies need to recognize that they are not part of the family and should not allow themselves to become too familiar with its members. When they disagree with the family on matters of raising the children, they should do so with tact and the realization that they are only employees. Finally, it is imperative that they be discreet about confidential family matters. A nanny who gossips about family affairs is likely to be rapidly dismissed.

EXPLORING

Babysitting is an excellent way to gain child-care experience. Often, a babysitter cares for children without any supervision, thereby learning child management and personal responsibility. Volunteer or part-time work at day care centers, nurseries, or elementary schools can also be beneficial.

Talk to a nanny to get further information. There are several placement agencies for prospective nannies, and one of them might be able to set up a meeting or phone interview with someone who works in the field.

Gather information about nannies either from the library or from sources listed at the end of this article.

EMPLOYERS

Mid- to upper-income parents who seek in-home child care for their children usually employ nannies. These opportunities are generally available across the country in large cities and affluent suburbs. Most nannies are placed in homes by placement agencies, by employment agencies, or through government-authorized programs.

STARTING OUT

Most schools that train nannies offer placement services. In addition, it is possible to register with an employment agency that places child-care workers. Currently, there are more than 200 agencies that specialize in placing nannies. Some agencies conduct recruitment drives or fairs to find applicants. Newspaper classified ads may also list job openings for nannies.

Prospective nannies should screen potential employers carefully. Applicants should ask for references from previous nannies, particularly if a family has had many prior nannies, and talk with one or more of them, if possible. There are many horror stories in nanny circles about past employers, and the prospective worker should not assume that every employer is exactly as he or she appears to be at first. Nannies also need to make sure that the specific duties and terms of the job are explicitly specified in a contract. Most agencies will supply sample contracts.

ADVANCEMENT

More than half of the nannies working in this country are under the age of 30. Many nannies work in child care temporarily as a way to support themselves through school. Many nannies leave their employers to start families of their own. Some nannies, as their charges grow older and start school, may be employed by a new family every few years. This may result in better-paying positions.

Other advancement opportunities for nannies depend on the personal initiative of the nanny. Some nannies enroll in college to get the necessary training to become teachers or child psychologists. Other nannies may establish their own child-care agencies or schools for nannies.

EARNINGS

A 2006 survey of nannies by the International Nanny Association found that 23 percent of respondents earned $15 an hour, 15 percent earned

$12 an hour, and 20 percent earned $10 an hour. A person earning these wages and working full time at 40 hours a week would have yearly incomes of $31,200, $24,960, and $20,800 respectively. The remaining 42 percent of survey respondents reported that their salary was based on factors such as their level of education and experience, the number of children they care for, and their geographic location.

In reality, however, nannies often work more than 40 hours per week, and their pay may not be based on an hourly rate, but rather be a flat amount that may range from $250 to $400 or more per week. These weekly earnings translate into yearly incomes ranging from $13,000 to $20,800 or more. Income also depends on such factors as the number of children, length of time with a family, and level of previous experience. Some employers provide room and board but in return offer lower pay. Presently, the highest demands for nannies are in large cities on the west and east coasts. High demand can result in higher wages.

Some nannies may be asked to travel with the family. If it is a business-oriented trip, a nanny may be compensated with wages as well as additional days off upon return. If the travel is for vacation, a nanny may get paid a bonus for working additional days. Some employers choose not to take their nannies along when they travel, and these nannies may not earn any wages while the family is gone. Such situations can be a financial disadvantage for the nanny who has been promised full-time work and full-time pay. It is recommended that nannies anticipate possible scenarios or situations that may affect their working schedules and wages and discuss these issues with employers in advance.

Nannies often have work contracts with their families that designate wages, requirements, fringe benefits, and salary increases. Health insurance, worker's compensation, and Social Security tax are sometimes included in the benefits package. Annual pay raises vary, with increases of 7 or 8 percent being on the high end of the scale.

WORK ENVIRONMENT

No other job involves as intimate a relationship with other people and their children as the nanny's job. Because nannies often live with their employers, it is important that they choose their employer with as much care as the employer chooses them. All necessary working conditions need to be negotiated at the time of hire. Nannies should be fair, flexible, and able to adapt to changes easily. Because nannies work in their employers' homes, their working conditions vary greatly. Some nannies are live-ins, sharing the home of their employer because of convenience or because of the number or age of children in the family. Newborn babies require additional care that may require the nanny to live on the premises.

It is also common for nannies to live with their families during the week and return to their homes on the weekends. When nannies live in the family's home, they usually have their own quarters or a small apartment that is separate from the rest of the family's bedrooms and offers some privacy. Sometimes the nanny's room is next to the children's room so it is possible for the nanny to respond immediately if help is needed.

Nannies who are not live-ins may expect to stay at the home for long periods of time, much longer than a traditional nine-to-five job. Since it often is the nanny's responsibility to put the children to bed in the evening, a nanny may not return home until late evening. Nannies are often asked to stay late or work weekends if the parents have other engagements.

The work of a nanny can be stressful or unpleasant. Many employers expect their nannies to do things unrelated to their job, such as clean the house, run errands, walk dogs, or babysit for neighborhood children. Some employers may be condescending, rude, and critical. Some mothers, while they need and want the services of a nanny, grow resentful and jealous of the bonds the nanny forms with the children.

Nannies have very few legal rights with regard to their jobs and have little recourse to deal with unfair employers. Job security is very poor, as parents have less need for nannies as their children get older and start school. In addition, nannies are often fired with no notice and sometimes no explanation due to the whims of their employers. Leaving behind a job and the children they have taken care of and grown close to can be emotionally difficult for workers in this field.

The work is often strenuous, requiring a great deal of lifting, standing, and walking or running. The work is also mentally taxing, as young children demand constant attention and energy. It can also be very rewarding for nannies as they grow close to the children, helping with their upbringing and care. In the best cases, the nanny becomes an integral part of the family he or she works for and is treated with professionalism, respect, and appreciation.

OUTLOOK

The U.S. Department of Labor predicts that employment for all child-care workers will grow about as fast as the average for all occupations through 2014. The department notes, however, that job opportunities for nannies should be particularly good. The continuing trend of both parents working outside the home ensures that nannies will remain in demand. Even if many of these parents switch to part-time jobs, there will still be a need for qualified child-care providers. Presently, the demand for nannies outweighs the supply, and graduating nannies may find themselves faced with several job offers. In addition, the long hours and low pay make for a high turnover rate in this field, and replacement workers are in steady demand. It may be years before the gap between the number of positions open and the availability of nannies diminishes.

FOR MORE INFORMATION

For information on educational standards and professional support, contact
American Council of Nanny Schools
Thirty South Franklin Street
Chagrin Falls, OH 44022-3213
Tel: 800-733-1984
Email: administration@nanny-governess.com
http://www.americancouncilofnannyschools.com

The following is an institution for the education and placement of certified professional nannies and certified professional governesses.
English Nanny and Governess School
37 South Franklin Street
Chagrin Falls, OH 44022-3212
Tel: 800-733-1984
Email: admissions@nanny-governess.com
http://www.nanny-governess.com

The following organization is an exchange program that places foreign students between the ages of 18 and 26 in American homes as au pairs for one year.
GoAuPair
151 East 6100 South, Suite 200
Murray, UT 84107-7489
Tel: 888-287-2471
Email: inforequest@goaupair.com
http://www.goaupair.com

For information on a career as a nanny and earnings, contact
International Nanny Association
2020 Southwest Freeway, Suite 208
Houston, TX 77098-4807
Tel: 888-878-1477
http://www.nanny.org

Personal Chefs

OVERVIEW

Personal chefs prepare menus for individuals and their families, purchase the ingredients for the meals, then cook, package, and store the meals in the clients' own kitchens. Approximately 5,000 personal chefs work across the United States and Canada, cooking for busy families, seniors, people with disabilities, and others who don't have the time or the ability to prepare meals for themselves.

HISTORY

Since the beginning of time, humans have experimented with food and cooking techniques in efforts to create simpler, quicker, more balanced meals. The development of pottery and agriculture was the earliest step toward better cooking, after years of using skulls and bones as cooking pots, and hunting for meat. Cooks have always built from the progress of previous generations; Catherine de Medicis of Italy is often credited with introducing, in the sixteenth century, masterful cooking to the French, where fine cuisine developed into an art form.

Though royalty, the famous, and the wealthy have long hired private chefs to work in their kitchens, personal chefs have only recently come onto the scene. Within the last 15 years, experienced cooks, either looking to expand their catering and restaurant businesses, or burnt-out from working as chefs, have begun meeting the demand for quick, easy meals that taste homemade. Men and women are holding down demanding, time-consuming jobs, and looking for alternatives to microwave dinners, fast food, and frozen pizzas. David MacKay founded the first professional association for personal chefs, the United States Personal

Chef Association (USPCA), in 1991, and helps to establish more than 400 new businesses every year. The American Personal Chef Association (APCA), founded by Candy Wallace, has also developed in recent years, offering training materials and certification to experienced cooks wanting to set up their own businesses.

THE JOB

What will you be cooking for dinner tonight? Spice-rubbed lamb chops with roasted tomatoes? Tarragon chicken with West Indian pumpkin soup? Or maybe turkey parmesan on a bed of red-pepper linguini? If you're rolling up your sleeves and ready to take on a variety of cooking challenges, then a personal chef service may be in your future. People without the time to cook, or without the ability, or those who just plain don't care to cook, are calling upon the services of chefs who will come into their kitchens, throw together delicious meals, then stack the meals in their freezers. A complete meal prepared according to the client's specifications is then only a few minutes of re-heating away.

A personal chef is usually someone with a great deal of cooking experience who, for a per-meal fee, will prepare enough meals to last a few days, or a few weeks, for individuals and their families. Personal chefs first meet with a new client to discuss special dietary needs and food preferences. Some clients require vegetarian and low-fat cooking; others have diabetes, or swallowing disorders that require special consideration. (If a personal chef has to do a great deal of research into a special diet plan, they might charge an additional consultation fee.) From these specifications, personal chefs prepare a menu. On the day that they'll be cooking the meals, they visit the grocery store to purchase fresh meats, fish, fruits, and vegetables. At the home of their client, they prepare the meals, package them, label them, and put them in the freezer. Depending on the number of meals, personal chefs spend anywhere from three to eight hours in their client's kitchen. Once they are done, they clean and move on to their next client. Personal chefs are able to control their work hours by limiting the number of clients they take on. They need between five and 10 regular clients to earn a full-time wage.

Most personal chefs prepare the meals in the kitchens of the clients, thereby avoiding the requirements of licensing their own kitchens for commercial use. Greg Porter, a personal chef in South Carolina, is an exception to this norm. As the owner of Masterchef Catering, he is able to prepare meals for his clients in his own commercial kitchen. He had been catering for four years when he began reading articles about personal cheffing. "I researched it on the Internet," he says, "and realized that I was already set up to do it."

Porter pursued training from the APCA and branched out into the business of personal chef. An article about him in an area newspaper resulted in five new clients. "I don't know of anyone else doing this in South Carolina," Porter says. He prepares upscale, gourmet meals for his clients, which can include "salmon, fresh steak, duck breast, rack of lamb, baby back ribs."

But cooking isn't the only talent needed for success in the personal chef business. They must also know meals and ingredients that can be easily frozen and reheated without hurting taste and appearance. They should have an understanding of nutrition, health, and sanitation. Good business sense is also important, as personal chefs need to keep financial records, market their service, and schedule and bill clients. They also need to test recipes, experiment with equipment, and look for the most cost-effective ways to purchase groceries. "APCA doesn't teach you how to cook," Porter says. "It shows you the ins and outs of the business."

Candy Wallace, the founder of APCA, developed the training course based on her own experiences as owner of "The Serving Spoon," a personal chef service. "The course is about personalizing service," she says, "as well as personalizing business to support your own well-being." Wallace has been in the business for more than five years. "I started by taking care of the little old ladies in my neighborhood," she says, referring to how she would drive elderly neighbors to their doctors' appointments, run errands for them, and help them prepare meals. She realized she could expand these services. She knew many people who were longing for the quality and nutrition of a home-cooked meal, but with the ease and speed of the less-healthy, chemical-laden frozen dinners. "I decided to design a program," she says, "for busy corporate women who didn't want their children to glow in the dark."

Most personal chefs try to confine their services to their local areas, or neighborhoods, to keep travel from kitchen to kitchen at a minimum. Sometimes, a good personal chef's services become so valuable to a client, the chef will be invited along on a family's vacation. "I've gone with clients to Palm Springs, Tahoe, Maui...," Wallace says.

REQUIREMENTS

High School
A home economics course can give you a good taste of what it's like to be a personal chef. You'll learn something about cooking, bud-

geting for groceries, and how to use various cooking equipment and appliances. A course in health will teach you about nutrition and a proper diet. Take a business course that offers lessons in bookkeeping and accounting to help you prepare for the record-keeping aspect of the job. A composition or communications course can help you develop the writing skills you'll need for self-promotion. Join a business organization for the chance to meet with small business owners, and to learn about the fundamentals of business operation.

Postsecondary Training

Both the APCA and the USPCA offer self-study courses and seminars on the personal chef business. These courses are not designed to teach people how to cook, but rather how to start a service, how to market it, how much to charge for services, and other concerns specific to the personal chef business. These courses also offer recipes for foods that freeze and store well.

A formal education isn't required of personal chefs, but a good culinary school can give you valuable cooking experience. "You must be well trained," Greg Porter advises. Porter holds an associate's degree in the culinary arts from the Johnson and Wales Culinary Institute, one of the highest-ranked cooking schools in the country. With a degree, you can pursue work in restaurants, hotels, health care facilities, and other industries needing the expertise of professional cooks. Culinary programs include courses in vegetarian cooking, menu design, food safety and sanitation, along with courses like economics and math. "But what will teach you more," Porter says, "is working part time for a restaurant, or a caterer, to learn the business. I've sold food, catered, managed, owned a restaurant—I've done it all, to learn the whole business inside out."

Certification or Licensing

To become a certified personal chef with the USPCA, you must work for at least two years as a personal chef. You're required to complete written and practical exams and meet educational requirements. The APCA, in conjunction with the American Culinary Federation, offers the personal certified chef designation to applicants who have at least four years of professional cooking experience, at least two years of employment as a personal chef, and who pass written and practical examinations. One quarter to one half of the personal chefs working in the United States and Canada are certified, but certification isn't required to work in the business.

Because you'll be working in the kitchens of your clients, you won't need licensing, or to adhere to the health department regulations of commercial kitchens. A few states, however, do charge permit fees, and require some inspections of the vehicle in which you carry groceries and cooking equipment.

Other Requirements

Porter emphasizes that a person should have an outgoing personality to be successful as a personal chef. "Customer service is the most important thing," he says. "If you're not people-oriented, you can just hang it up." A strong work ethic and an ambition to succeed are also very important—you'll be promoting your business, building a client list, and handling administrative details all yourself. You'll need patience, too, not only as you prepare quality meals, but also as you wait for your business to develop and your client list to grow. You should be a creative thinker, capable of designing interesting menus within the specifications of the client. And, of course, keep in mind that you'll be cooking several meals a day, every day. So it may not be enough to just "like" cooking; you'll need a passion for it.

EXPLORING

The most valuable exploration you can do is to spend time in the kitchen. Learn how to properly use the cooking appliances and utensils. Experiment with recipes; various Web posting sites include recipes that are good to freeze and store. This way you'll learn what meals would work best in a personal chef service. Cook for friends and family, and volunteer to work at high school banquets and soup kitchens. Contact the professional associations for names of personal chefs in your area. Some chefs participate in mentoring programs to help people learn about the business. Look into part-time work with a restaurant, cafe, or caterer. Many caterers hire assistants on a temporary basis to help with large events.

EMPLOYERS

Nearly all personal chef services are owned and operated by individuals, though some well-established chefs serving a largely populated, affluent area may hire assistants. Aspiring personal chefs who live in one of these areas and have some cooking experience and education may be able to hire on as a cook with a big personal chef operation. But most personal chefs will be in business for themselves and will promote their services in areas near their home.

The majority of people who use the services of personal chefs are working couples that have household incomes over $70,000. Most of these couples have children. Personal chefs also work for people with disabilities and senior citizens. "A lot of clients are seniors," Candy Wallace of APCA says. "They want to stay in their own homes, but never want to see the inside of a grocery store or a kitchen again. Some of these clients are in their 90s."

STARTING OUT

David MacKay, founder of USPCA, emphasizes that the career of personal chef is really for those who have tried other careers and have some experience in the food and service industry. The personal chef courses being offered by USPCA-accredited community colleges may eventually change this and may draw people with little cooking experience into the business. For now, though, a personal chef course and seminar isn't really enough to get you started unless you also have a culinary education, or a great deal of knowledge about cooking.

If you feel confident that you have the cooking knowledge necessary to prepare good-tasting, well-balanced meals for paying customers, then you should consider training through either APCA or USPCA. Once you have a good sense of the requirements and demands of the job, you can start seeking out clients. Because you'll be cooking with the stoves and appliances of your clients, you don't need to invest much money into starting up your business. An initial investment of about $1,000 will buy you some quality cookware and utensils. But you'll also need a reliable vehicle, as you'll be driving to the grocery store and to the homes of your clients every day.

Volunteer your services for a week or two to friends and neighbors who you think might be interested in hiring you. Print up some fliers and cards, and post your name on community bulletin boards. You may have to offer a low, introductory price to entice clients to try your services.

ADVANCEMENT

Most personal chefs only cook for one or two clients daily, so maintaining between five and 10 clients will keep them pretty busy. If a personal chef is able to attract many more customers than they can handle, it may be beneficial for them to hire assistants and to raise their prices. As they grow their business, personal chefs may choose to expand into other areas, like catering large events, writing food-related articles for a local newspaper or magazine, or teaching cooking classes. They may also meet with owners of grocery stores and restaurants, consulting with them about developing their own meal take-out services.

EARNINGS

According to the USPCA, salaries for personal chefs range from about $35,000 annually on the low end to $50,000 on the high end. Some chefs with assistant cooks and a number of clients can make much more than that, but businesses composed of a single owner/ operator average about $40,000 per year.

Personal chefs usually sell their services as a package deal—typically $250 to $300 for 10 meals for two people, with a fee of $10 to $15 for each additional meal. A complete package may take a full day to prepare. This may seem like a very good wage, but it's important to remember that personal chefs must pay for the groceries. Though they will be able to save some money by buying staples in bulk, and by planning their menus efficiently, they'll also be spending a lot on fresh meat, fish, and vegetables. One-third or less of a personal chef's 10-meal package fee will go toward the expense of its ingredients.

WORK ENVIRONMENT

Greg Porter likes the "personal" aspect of working as a personal chef. "My customers become friends," he says. He appreciates being able to prepare meals based on the individual tastes of his customers, rather than "the 300 people coming into a restaurant." Many personal chefs enter the business after burning out on the demands of restaurant work. Many enjoy making their own schedule, avoiding the late nights, long hours, and weekends of restaurant service.

Though personal chefs don't work in their own homes, they don't travel that much. They will have to visit a grocery store every morning for fresh meats and produce, but most of the hours of each workday will be spent in one or two kitchens. Freezer space, pantries, and stoves obviously won't be as large as those in a commercial kitchen, but work spaces are generally more inviting and homey than those in the back of a restaurant. Personal chefs work entirely on their own, with little supervision by their clients. In most cases, their clients will be at work, allowing them to create their meals, and their messes, in private.

OUTLOOK

The personal chef industry is growing in leaps and bounds, and will continue to do so. The career has become recognized by culinary institutes, and some schools are beginning to include personal chef courses as part of their curriculums. The national publications *Entrepreneur, Time, US News and World Report*, and others have listed personal chef services as one of the hottest new businesses.

Though the basics of the job will likely remain the same in future years, it is subject to some trends. Personal chefs will need to keep up with diet fads and new health concerns, as well as trends in gourmet cooking. As the career gains prominence, states may regulate it more rigorously, requiring certain health inspections and permits. Some states may also begin to require special food safety and sanitation training.

FOR MORE INFORMATION

For information on certification for personal chefs, contact
American Culinary Federation Inc.
180 Center Place Way
St. Augustine, FL 32095-8859
Tel: 800-624-9458
http://www.acfchefs.org

The APCA holds seminars, offers certification, and maintains an informative Web site with a personal chef message board.
American Personal Chef Association (APCA)
4572 Delaware Street
San Diego, CA 92116-1005
Tel: 800-644-8389
Email: contact@personalchef.com
http://www.personalchef.com

The USPCA offers training courses, certification, and mentorship.
United States Personal Chef Association (USPCA)
610 Quantum Road NE
Rio Rancho, NM 87124
Tel: 800-995-2138
http://www.uspca.com

INTERVIEW

Lauren Cahoon is the owner of An Artful Palate in Chicago, Illinois. She discussed her career with the editors of Careers in Focus: Personal Services.

Q. Please tell us about yourself and your business.

A. I am 26 years old and started my personal chef business in 2006. Prior to becoming a personal chef, I was working full time in public relations but knew that cooking was my true passion. I knew I wanted a culinary career, but I did not want the long and irregular hours of working in a restaurant, so I started doing some research into the rapidly growing personal chef industry and found it to be a perfect fit for my skills and goals. As a personal chef, I plan menus, grocery shop, and prepare fresh meals for my clients to reheat at their convenience.

Q. Please briefly describe your primary and secondary job responsibilities.

A. My primary responsibilities include planning weekly and biweekly menus based on my clients' dietary needs and preferences, grocery shopping to buy all the fresh ingredients needed to prepare these menus, and cooking and packaging the food in the client's home so that it can be reheated later. I also leave them with detailed reheating instructions for the oven or microwave. My secondary job responsibility is to find new ways to market my business to potential clients.

Q. As a new personal chef, what have been the most challenging aspects of starting a new business?

A. Finding clients is the biggest challenge. Many people don't know what a personal chef does, or they think we only cook for the rich and famous. However, I've learned that any encounter with a new person is a potential marketing opportunity, so when meeting people, I'm always analyzing whether they might benefit from my service and always have my sales pitch ready.

Q. What advice would you offer young people who are interested in the field?

A. Do your research and network as much as possible. Most states and larger cities have local personal chef organizations that can be a great resource for learning about the industry and meeting others who are already running successful personal chef businesses. I would also recommend shadowing a personal chef for a day to get firsthand experience of what we do on a daily basis.

Personal Shoppers

OVERVIEW

People who don't have the time or the ability to go shopping for clothes, gifts, groceries, and other items use the services of *personal shoppers*. Personal shoppers shop in department stores, look at catalogs, and surf the Internet for the best buys and most appropriate items for their clients. Relying on a sense of style and an ability to spot a bargain, a personal shopper helps clients develop a wardrobe and find gifts for friends, relatives, and employees. Though personal shoppers work across the country, their services are in most demand in large, metropolitan areas.

HISTORY

For decades, American retailers have been working to create easier ways to shop. Mail-order was an early innovation: catalog companies such as Montgomery Wards and Sears, Roebuck and Co. started business in the late 19th century to meet the shopping needs of people living in rural areas and small towns. Many consumers relied on mail-order for everything from suits and dresses to furniture and stoves; Sears even sold automobiles through the mail. Shopping for food, clothes, and gifts was considered a household chore, a responsibility that belonged to women. By the late 1800s, shopping had developed into a popular pastime in metropolitan areas. Wealthy women of leisure turned downtown shopping districts into the busiest sections of their cities, as department stores, boutiques, tea shops, and cafes evolved to serve them.

As more women joined the workforce after World War II, retailers worked to make their shopping areas more convenient. Supermarkets, shopping centers, and malls became popular. Toward the end of the 20th century, shoppers began looking for even more simplicity and convenience. In the 1990s, many companies began to market their products via the Internet. In addition to Internet commerce, overworked men and women are turning to personal shoppers, professional organizers, and personal assistants to fulfill their shopping needs.

THE JOB

Looking for a job where you get to shop all the time, tell people what to wear, and spend somebody else's money? Though this may seem to describe the life of the personal shopper, it's not quite accurate. For one thing, personal shoppers don't get to shop all the time; they will be spending some time in stores and browsing catalogs, but they're often looking for something very specific and working as quickly as they can. And they do not so much tell people what to wear as teach them how to best match outfits, what colors suit them, and what styles are most appropriate for their workplaces. Yes, personal shoppers spend someone else's money, but it's all for someone else's closet. So, if you're not too disillusioned, read on: working as a personal shopper may still be right for you.

Personal shoppers help people who are unable or uninterested in doing their own shopping. They are hired to look for that perfect gift for a difficult-to-please aunt. They work for senior citizens, or people with disabilities, to do their grocery shopping and run other shopping errands. Personal shoppers help professionals create a nice, complete wardrobe. All the while, they rely on their knowledge of the local marketplace in order to do the shopping quickly and efficiently.

Some personal shoppers use their backgrounds in other areas to assist clients. Those with a background in cosmetology may work as *image consultants,* advising clients on their hair, clothes, and makeup. Some shoppers may have some experience in dealing antiques and will help clients locate particular items. Interior decorators may shop for furniture and art to decorate a home.

Personal shoppers who offer wardrobe consultation will need to visit their client's home and evaluate his or her clothes. They help their clients determine what additional clothes and accessories they'll need, and they offer advice on which jackets to wear with which pants, or which skirt to wear with which blouse. Together with their client, personal shoppers determine what additional clothes are needed to complete the wardrobe, and they come up with a budget. Then it's off to the stores.

Irene Kato owns I Kan Do It Personal Shopper, Etc., a personal shopping service. She offers a variety of services, including at-home wardrobe consultation, closet organization, and gift-shopping. "Most of my shopping so far has been for clothes," Kato says. "I have a fairly good idea of what I'm looking for, so I don't spend too much time in any one store if I don't see what I want right away. I can usually find two or three choices for my client and rarely have to shop another day." Kato spends about two to three hours every other day shopping, and about two hours a day in her office working on publicity, her budget, and corresponding with clients. Shopping for one client can take about three hours. "I have always enjoyed shopping," Kato says, "and especially like finding bargains. Waiting in lines, crowds, etc., does not bother me."

Personal shoppers often cater to professionals needing business attire and wardrobe consultation. A smaller part of their business will be shopping for gifts. They may even supplement their business by running other errands, such as purchasing theater tickets, making deliveries, and going to the post office. Many personal shoppers also work as *professional organizers:* they go into homes and offices to organize desks, kitchens, and closets.

In addition to the actual shopping, personal shoppers have administrative responsibilities. They must keep business records, make phone calls, and schedule appointments. Since personal shopping is a fairly new endeavor, personal shoppers must be experts at educating the public about their services. "A personal shopper has no commodity to sell," Kato says, "only themselves. So it is twice as hard to attract clients." To publicize her business, Kato maintains a Web site (http://www.ikandoit.net) that lists the services she provides and testimonials from clients. She also belongs to two professional organizations that help her network and develop her business: Executive Women International and Giving Referrals to Other Women.

REQUIREMENTS

High School

Take classes in home economics to develop budget and consumer skills as well as learn about fashion and home design. If the class offers a sewing unit, you'll learn about tailoring, and you can develop an eye for clothing sizes. Math, business, and accounting courses will prepare you for the administrative details of the job. English composition and speech classes will help you develop the communication skills you'll need to promote your business and advise clients about their wardrobes.

Postsecondary Training

Many professional personal shoppers have had experience in other areas of business. They've worked as managers in corporations or have worked as salespeople in retail stores. But because of the entrepreneurial nature of the career, you don't need any specific kind of education or training. A small-business course at your local community college, along with classes in design, fashion, and consumer science, can help you develop the skills you'll need for the job. If you're unfamiliar with the computer, you should take some classes to learn desktop publishing programs for creating business cards and other publicity material.

Other Requirements

"I seem to have an empathy for people," Irene Kato says. "After talking with a client, I know what they want and what they're looking for. I am a very good listener." In addition to these people skills, a personal shopper should be patient and capable of dealing with the long lines and customer service of department stores. You should be creative and able to come up with a variety of gift ideas. A sense of style is important, along with knowledge of the latest brands and designers. You'll need a good eye for colors and fabrics. You should also be well dressed and organized so that your client will know to trust your wardrobe suggestions.

EXPLORING

If you've spent any time at the mall, you probably already have enough shopping experience. And if you've had to buy clothes and gifts with limited funds, then you know something about budgeting. Sign up for the services of a personal shopper in a department store; in most stores the service is free, and you'll get a sense of how a shopper works. Pay close attention to the information they request from you in the beginning, then ask them later about their decision-making process. Irene Kato advises future personal shoppers to work a few years at a retail clothing store. "This way," she says, "you can observe the way people dress, what shapes and sizes we all are, how fashion trends come and go, and what stays."

EMPLOYERS

Professional men and women with high incomes and busy schedules are the primary employers of personal shoppers. Shoppers may also work with people with new jobs requiring dress clothes, but also with people who need to perk up an old wardrobe. Personal shoppers may work for executives in corporations who need to buy gifts for large staffs of employees. Some of their clients may be elderly or have disabilities and have problems getting out to do their shopping.

STARTING OUT

Start-up costs for personal shoppers can be very low; you may only have to invest in a computer, business cards, and a reliable form of transportation. But it could take you a very long time to develop a regular clientele. You'll want to develop the business part time while still working full time at another, more reliable job. Some of your first clients may come from your workplace. Offer free introductory services to a few people and encourage them to spread the word and hand out your business card. You'll also need to become very familiar with the local retail establishments and the discount stores with low-cost, high-quality merchandise.

"My friends and colleagues at work," Irene Kato says, "were always complimentary on what I wore and would ask where I bought my clothes, where they could find certain items, where were the best sales." Kato was taking the part-time approach to developing her personal shopping service, when downsizing at her company thrust her into the new business earlier than she'd planned. She had the opportunity to take an entrepreneurism class at a local private university, which helped her devise a business plan and taught her about the pros and cons of starting a business.

ADVANCEMENT

It takes years of dedication, quality work, and referrals to create a successful business. Personal shoppers should expect lean, early years as they work to build their business and expand their clientele. After a few years of working part time and providing superior service, a personal shopper may develop his or her business into a full-time endeavor. Eventually, he or she may be able to hire an assistant to help with the administrative work, such as client billing and scheduling.

EARNINGS

Personal shoppers bill their clients in different ways: they set a regular fee for services, charge a percentage of the sale, or charge an hourly rate. They might use all of these methods in their business;

their billing method may depend on the client and the service. For example, when offering wardrobe consultation and shopping for clothes, a personal shopper may find it best to charge by the hour; when shopping for a small gift, it may be more reasonable to charge only a percentage. Personal shoppers charge anywhere from $25 to $125 an hour; the average hourly rate is about $75. Successful shoppers living in a large city can make between $1,500 and $3,000 a month.

WORK ENVIRONMENT

Personal shoppers have all the advantages of owning their own business, including setting their own hours and keeping a flexible schedule. But they also have all the disadvantages, such as job insecurity and lack of benefits. "I have a bad habit of thinking about my business almost constantly," Irene Kato says. Though personal shoppers don't have to deal with the stress of a full-time office job, they will have the stress of finding new clients and keeping the business afloat entirely by themselves.

Although personal shoppers usually work from a home office, they still spend a lot of time with people, from clients to salespeople. They will obviously spend some time in department stores; if they like to shop, this can be enjoyable, even when they're not buying anything for themselves. In some cases, personal shoppers visit clients' homes to advise them on their wardrobe. They do a lot of traveling, driving to a department store after a meeting with a client, and then back to the client's with the goods.

OUTLOOK

Personal shopping is a new business development, so anyone embarking on the career will be taking some serious risks. There's not a lot of research available about the career, no national professional organization specifically serving personal shoppers, and no real sense of the career's future. The success of Internet commerce will probably have a big effect on the future of personal shopping. If purchasing items through the Internet becomes more commonplace, personal shoppers may have to establish places for themselves on the World Wide Web. Some personal shoppers currently with Web sites offer consultation via e-mail and help people purchase products online.

To attract the widest variety of clients, personal shoppers should offer as expansive a service as they can. Professional organizing is being recognized as one of the top home businesses for the future;

membership of the National Association of Professional Organizers is growing each year. *Personal assistants,* those who run errands for others, have also caught the attention of industry experts, and programs are available to assist people interested in entering this field.

FOR MORE INFORMATION

For more information on professional networking opportunities for women, contact
Executive Women International
515 South 700 East, Suite 2A
Salt Lake City, UT 84102-2855
Tel: 801-355-2800
Email: ewi@executivewomen.org
http://www.executivewomen.org

To learn about a career as a professional organizer, contact
National Association of Professional Organizers
4700 West Lake Avenue
Glenview, IL 60025-1468
Tel: 847-375-4746
Email: hq@napo.net
http://www.napo.net

Personal Trainers

OVERVIEW

Personal trainers, often known as *fitness trainers,* assist health-conscious people with exercise, weight training, weight loss, diet and nutrition, and medical rehabilitation. During one training session, or over a period of several sessions, trainers teach their clients how to achieve their health and fitness goals. They train in the homes of their clients, their own studio spaces, or in health clubs. More than 65,000 personal trainers work in the United States, either independently or on the staff of a fitness center.

HISTORY

For much of the last half of the 20th century, "98-pound weaklings" were tempted by the Charles Atlas comic book ads to buy his workout plan and to bulk up. Atlas capitalized on a concern for good health that developed into the fitness industry after World War II. Though physical fitness has always been important to the human body, things have changed quite a bit since the days when people had to chase and hunt their own food. Before the industrial revolution, people were much more active, and the need for supplemental exercise was unnecessary. But the last century has brought easier living, laziness, and processed snack foods.

Even as early as the late 1800s, people became concerned about their health and weight and began to flock to spas and exercise camps. This proved to be a passing fad for the most part, but medical and nutritional study began to carefully explore the significance of exercise. During World War II, rehabilitation medicine proved more effective than extended rest in returning soldiers to the front line. Even the early days of TV featured many morning segments devoted to exercise. The videotape revolution of the 1980s went hand in hand with a new fitness craze, as Jane Fonda's workout tape became a bestseller and inspired a whole industry of fitness tapes and books. Now, most health clubs offer the services of personal trainers to attend to the health and fitness concerns of its members.

THE JOB

Remember the first time you ever went to the gym? The weight machines may have resembled medieval forms of torture. So, to avoid the weight training, you stuck to the treadmill. Or maybe you called upon the services of a personal trainer. Personal trainers help their clients achieve health and fitness goals. They instruct on the proper use of exercise equipment and weight machines and may suggest diet and nutrition tips.

If you've reached your own workout goals, then you may be ready to help others reach theirs. "You have to believe in working out and eating healthy," advises Emelina Edwards, a personal trainer in New Orleans. For 12 years she's been in the business of personal training, a career she chose after whipping herself into great shape at the age of 46. Now, at 58, she has a lot of first-hand experience in training, nutrition, aerobic exercise, and stress management. Edwards says, "You have to practice what you preach."

And practice Edwards does—not only does she devote time every day to her own weight training, jogging, and meditation, but she works with three to five clients in the workout facility in her home. She has a total of about 20 clients, some of whom she assists in one-on-one sessions, and others in small groups. Her clients have included men and women from the ages of 20 to 80 who are looking to improve their general physical condition or to work on specific ailments.

When meeting with a client for the first time, Edwards gets a quick history of his or her physical problems and medical conditions. "If problems are serious," Edwards says, "I check with their doctor. If mild, I explain to them what I believe will help." When she discovered that four out of five people seeking her help suffered from back problems, she did a great deal of research on back pain and how to alleviate it through exercise. "I teach people how to do for themselves," she says. "Sometimes I see a person once, or for three or four sessions, or forever."

In addition to working directly with clients, Edwards is active promoting her line of "Total Body Rejuvenation" products. These

A personal trainer encourages his client during an exercise. *(Paul Audia, Index Stock Imagery)*

products, consisting of audiotapes and books, are based on her years of experience and the many articles she has written for fitness publications. When she's not training clients, writing articles, and selling products, she's reading fitness publications to keep up on the business, as well as speaking at public events. "When I realized I loved training," she says, "I thought of all the things I could relate to it. So along with the training, I began to write about it, and to give talks on health and fitness."

Successful personal trainers don't necessarily have to keep as busy as Edwards. They may choose to specialize in certain areas of personal training. They may work as an *athletic trainer,* helping athletes prepare for sports activities. They may specialize in helping with the rehabilitation treatment of people with injuries and other physical problems. Yoga, dance, martial arts, indoor cycling, boxing, and water fitness have all become aspects of special training programs. People call upon personal trainers to help them quit smoking, to assist with healthy pregnancies, and to maintain mental and emotional stability. Whatever the problem, whether mental or physical, people are turning to exercise and nutrition to help them deal with it.

Many personal trainers have their own studios or home gyms where they train their clients; others go into the homes of their clients. Because of the demands of the workplace, many personal trainers also work in offices and corporate fitness centers. Though most health clubs hire their own trainers to assist with club members, some hire freelance trainers as independent contractors. These independent contractors are not considered staff members and don't receive employee benefits. (IDEA Health and Fitness Association found that 30 percent of the personal trainers hired by the fitness centers surveyed were independent contractors.)

REQUIREMENTS

High School

If you're interested in health and fitness, you're probably already taking physical education classes and involved in sports activities. It's also important to take health courses and courses like home economics, which include lessons in diet and nutrition. Business courses can help you prepare for the management aspect of running your own personal training service. Science courses such as biology, chemistry, and physiology are important for your understanding of muscle groups, food and drug reactions, and other concerns of exercise science. If you're not interested in playing on sports teams, you may be able to volunteer as an assistant. These positions will allow you to learn about athletic training as well as rehabilitation treatments.

Postsecondary Training

A college education isn't required to work as a personal trainer, but you can benefit from one of the many fitness-related programs offered at colleges across the country. Some relevant college programs include health education, exercise and sports science, fitness program management, and athletic training. These programs include courses in therapeutic exercise, nutrition, aerobics, and fitness and aging. IDEA recommends a bachelor's degree from a program that includes at least a semester each in anatomy, kinesiology, and exercise physiology. IDEA offers scholarships to students seeking careers as fitness professionals.

If you're not interested in a full four-year program, many schools offer shorter versions of their bachelor's programs. Upon completing a shorter program, you'll receive either an associate's degree or certification from the school. Once you've established yourself in the business, continuing education courses are important for you to keep up with the advances in the industry. IDEA is one of many organizations that offer independent study courses, conferences, and seminars.

Certification or Licensing

There are so many schools and organizations that offer certification to personal trainers that it has become a concern in the industry. Without more rigid standards, the profession could suffer at the hands of less experienced, less skilled trainers. Some organizations only require membership fees and short tests for certification. Emelina Edwards isn't certified and doesn't believe that certification is necessary. "Experience is what counts," she says.

But some health clubs look for certified trainers when hiring independent contractors. If you are seeking certification, you should choose a certifying board that offers scientifically based exams and requires continuing education credits. The American Council on Exercise, the National Federation of Professional Trainers, and the American Fitness Professionals and Associates are just a few of the many groups with certification programs.

Other Requirements

Physical fitness and knowledge of health and nutrition are the most important assets of personal trainers. "The more intelligently you can speak to someone," Edwards says, "the more receptive they'll be." Your clients will also be more receptive to patience and friendliness. "I'm very enthusiastic and positive," she says, regarding the way she works with her clients. You should be able to explain things clearly, recognize progress, and encourage it. You should be comfortable working one-on-one with people of all ages and in all physical conditions. An interest in reading fitness books and publications is important to your continuing education.

EXPLORING

Your high school may have a weight-training program, or some other extracurricular fitness program, as part of its athletic department; in addition to signing up for the program, you can assist the faculty who manage it. That way, you can learn about what goes into developing and maintaining such a program. If your school doesn't have a fitness program, seek one out at a community center, or join a health club.

You should also try the services of a personal trainer. By conditioning yourself and eating a healthy diet, you'll get a good sense of the duties of a personal trainer. Any number of books and magazines address issues of health and nutrition and offer weight-training advice. IDEA publishes several helpful health- and career-related publications, including *IDEA Fitness Journal* and *IDEA Trainer Success.*

Finally, seek out part-time work at a gym or health club to meet trainers and learn about weight machines and certification programs.

EMPLOYERS

IDEA reports that there are more than 65,000 personal trainers working in the United States. Personal trainers are employed by people of all ages. Individuals hire the services of trainers, as do companies for the benefit of their employees. Though most health clubs hire personal trainers full time, some clubs hire trainers on an independent contractor basis. Sports and exercise programs at community colleges hire trainers part time to conduct classes.

Personal trainers can find clients in most major cities in all regions of the country. In addition to health clubs and corporate fitness centers, trainers find work at YMCAs, aerobics studios, and hospital fitness centers.

STARTING OUT

Most people who begin personal training do so after successful experiences with their own training. Once they've developed a good exercise regimen and healthy diet plan for themselves, they may feel ready to help others. Emelina Edwards had hit a low point in her life, and had turned to weight training to help her get through the difficult times. "I didn't have a college degree," she says, "and I needed something to do. All I had was weight training." She then called up all the women she knew, promoting her services as a personal trainer. Through the benefit of word-of-mouth, Edwards built up a clientele.

Some trainers begin by working part time or full time for health clubs and, after making connections, they go into business for themselves. As with most small businesses, personal trainers must promote themselves through classified ads, flyers posted in community centers, and other forms of advertisement. Many personal trainers have published guides on how to establish businesses. IDEA offers a book called *The Successful Trainer's Guide to Marketing: How to Get Clients and Make Money,* which offers advice on how to attract clients.

ADVANCEMENT

After personal trainers have taken on as many individual clients as they need to maintain a business, they may choose to lead small, group training sessions or conduct large aerobics classes. Some trainers join forces with other trainers to start their own fitness centers. Trainers who are employed by fitness centers may be promoted to the position of *personal training director*. These workers supervise and schedule other personal trainers and manage department budgets.

Emelina Edwards has advanced her business by venturing out into other areas of fitness instruction, such as publishing books and speaking to groups. "I want to develop more in the public speaking arena," she says. Right now, she only speaks to local groups—she'd like to go national. "I'd also like to break into the Latin market," she says. "The interest is there, and the response has been great."

EARNINGS

IDEA reports that the average hourly rate for personal trainers is $41. Hourly fees ranged from less than $20 to $70 or more. Personal trainers who offer specialized instruction (such as in yoga, martial arts, or indoor cycling), or who work with their own clients in their own homes, can charge higher hourly rates.

WORK ENVIRONMENT

Personal training is obviously a physically demanding job, but anybody who is in good shape and who eats a healthy diet should be able to easily handle the demands. Personal trainers who work out of their homes will enjoy familiar and comfortable surroundings. Trainers who work in a gym as independent contractors will also experience a comfortable workplace. Most good gyms maintain a cool temperature, keep the facilities clean and well lit, and care for the weight machines. Whether in a gym or at home, personal trainers work directly with their clients, usually in one-on-one training sessions. In this teaching situation, the workplace is usually quiet and conducive to learning.

As with most self-employment, sustaining a business can be both rewarding and difficult. Many trainers appreciate being able to keep their own hours, and to work as little, or as much, as they care to. By setting their own schedules, they can arrange time for their personal workout routines. But, without an employer, there's less security, no benefits, and no steady paycheck. Personal trainers have to regularly promote their services and be ready to take on new clients.

OUTLOOK

Fitness training will continue to enjoy strong growth in the near future. As the baby boomers grow older, they will increasingly rely on the services of personal trainers. Boomers have long been interested in health and fitness, and they'll carry this into their old age. Knowledge of special weight training, stretching exercises, and diets for seniors will be necessary for personal trainers in the years to come. Trainers will actively promote their services to senior centers and retirement communities.

With the number of health publications and fitness centers, people are much more knowledgeable about exercise and nutrition. This could increase business for personal trainers, as people better understand the necessity of proper training and seek out professional assistance. Trainers may also be going into more of their clients' homes as people set up their own workout stations complete with weights and treadmills. In the health and medical field, new developments are constantly affecting how people eat and exercise. Personal trainers must keep up with these advances, as well as any new trends in fitness and dieting.

FOR MORE INFORMATION

For general health and fitness topics, and to learn about certification, contact

American Council on Exercise
4851 Paramount Drive
San Diego, CA 92123-1449
Tel: 800-825-3636
http://www.acefitness.org

For information on certification, contact

American Fitness Professionals and Associates
PO Box 214
Ship Bottom, NJ 08008-0234
Tel: 800-494-7782
Email: afpa@afpafitness.com
http://www.afpafitness.com

IDEA conducts surveys, provides continuing education, and publishes a number of books and magazines relevant to personal trainers. For information about the fitness industry in general, and personal training specifically, contact

IDEA Health and Fitness Association
10455 Pacific Center Court
San Diego, CA 92121-4339
http://www.ideafit.com

For information on certification, contact
National Federation of Professional Trainers
PO Box 4579
Lafayette, IN 47903-4579
Tel: 800-729-6378
http://www.nfpt.com

Pest Control Workers

OVERVIEW

Pest control workers treat residential and commercial properties with chemicals and mechanical traps to get rid of rodents, insects, and other common pests. They may work for a pest control company, lawn or landscaping firms, or own and operate their own company. Pest control workers make periodic visits to their clients' properties to make sure they remain pest-free. They may also use chemicals to control diseases and pests that attack lawns, shrubs, and other outdoor vegetation. There are approximately 68,000 pest control workers in the United States.

HISTORY

Pest control as an industry is a fairly recent development. In earlier times, fumigators were often brought into houses where someone had suffered a highly contagious disease, such as smallpox, to rid the house of germs. The most common method of banishing germs was to burn a large amount of an antiseptic that was a highly corrosive substance, such as sulfur. This practice was dangerous to humans, however, and often damaged furniture and household goods.

As scientists researched and tested chemicals, it was discovered that the application of certain chemicals as a method of controlling pests in homes and offices was effective. Chemical research in the 20th century made possible the use of a variety of substances that are toxic to pests but not harmful to people, pets, or household furnishings, when they are used in the proper quantities.

The use of specially trained pest control technicians arose from this need for precision and knowledge in the application of treatments, and today, the pest control industry does billions of dollars a year in business.

THE JOB

The majority of pest control workers are employed as *exterminators* or *pest control technicians*. These workers travel to homes, restaurants, hotels, food stores, warehouses, and other places where pests are likely to live and breed. Before starting on their route, they load their truck with pesticides, sprayers, and other necessary equipment, and obtain route slips from company offices showing the customers' names and addresses, services to be performed, and inspection comments. Once at the residence to be serviced, they inspect the premises for rodent droppings, physical damage from insects, and other signs of infestation. They then apply chemical sprays for flies, roaches, beetles, silverfish, and other household insects in cracks in floors and walls, under sinks, and in other places that provide shelter for these pests. Mechanical traps are set for rodents, and poisonous bait is left for them in areas where it will not contaminate food supplies or endanger children or pets.

Sometimes the pest infestation in a house requires the pest control worker to resort to fogging, which involves using a vapor that contains a very small amount of pesticide. This fog penetrates the different places where pests hide. Before fogging, the homeowners must leave for a short while, taking any pets with them. The pest control worker, often known as a *fumigator*, then begins to spray a fine pesticide mist that will not leave deposits on fabrics or flat surfaces. The worker wears a mask or respirator and protective clothing during this procedure. This mist is applied starting in the rear of the house and continuing until the worker exits through the front door. After a certain amount of time, the residents can safely return.

Many commercial establishments have service contracts with an exterminating company that sends workers on a biweekly, monthly, or quarterly basis to make sure the premises remain free of pests. Workers often use a concept known as "integrated pest management" with these customers, which involves advising them on housekeeping and home repair methods to keep pests from returning.

A smaller percentage of pest control workers are *termite exterminators*, and they perform a more extensive and complicated job than other workers in the industry do. Termites are particularly destructive pests. Their appetite for wood causes up to $2 billion a year in

A pest control worker sprays pesticide beneath a kitchen sink. *(Jim Whitmer Photography)*

property damage. Termite exterminators treat termites, which live in underground colonies and eat away the foundations and structural parts of wooden houses, by laying down a chemical barrier between the termite colony and the structure. This barrier traps the termites either underground, where there is no wood to eat, or in the walls, where they cannot find water. Eventually, the colony dies of either starvation or dehydration. Another method of treating termite infestation involves pumping gaseous pesticides into buildings that have been sealed or covered by tarpaulins.

Termite exterminators must sometimes make structural changes to the buildings they service. Holes may have to be drilled in basement floors to pump chemicals into the soil under the house. To keep termites from returning, exterminators must sometimes raise foundations or replace infested wood. If this alteration work is very extensive, however, the homeowner usually calls in building contractors and carpenters. Once termites have been thoroughly eradicated from a building, they are not likely to return soon. For this reason, termite exterminators work on a single-visit rather than a contract basis. The work of several exterminators may be directed and coordinated by an *extermination supervisor.*

In addition to the above duties, pest control workers must keep records of the dates each account is serviced, the type and strength

Did You Know?

- There are more than 12,000 species of ants in the world.
- Approximately 12,000 different kinds of beetles exist in the United States alone.
- Cockroaches are one of the oldest insects in the world. Their fossils have been dated as far back as 200 million years.
- Fleas can jump up to 120 times the length of their bodies.
- There are more than 120,000 species of flies in the world.
- Mice eat 15 to 20 times a day.
- Some types of moths have natural antifreeze in their bodies that allow them to stay active during cold weather.
- Termites eat constantly—24 hours a day, seven days a week. Like cockroaches, they are some of the oldest insects in the world.
- There are 4,000 species of wasps in the United States.
- Rats can chew through glass, wire, cinderblock, aluminum, and lead.

Source: PestWorld for Kids

of pesticides used, and any reported pest problems. They may also be responsible for collecting payment on accounts.

REQUIREMENTS

High School
The minimum requirement for pest control occupations is a high school diploma. A college degree is not required, although nearly half of all pest controllers have attended college or earned a degree. High school classes such as vocational-technical, earth science, math, writing, and chemistry would be beneficial to people who want to work in this profession.

Postsecondary Training
Pest controllers usually begin as apprentices when they learn pesticide safety and use. At this time, they also train in one or more of several pest control categories, such as nuisance pest control, wood preservation and treatment, rodent control, termite control, fumigation, and ornamental and turf control. Training includes approximately 10 hours in the classroom and 60 hours on the job for each specialty. Apprentices have up to one year to prepare for and pass the written examinations, after which they become licensed technicians.

Certification or Licensing

Under the Federal Insecticide, Fungicide, and Rodenticide Act, all pesticide products are classified by the degree of hazard they pose to people and the environment. Therefore, pest control workers must be licensed in all states. Some of these states also require the applicant to pass a written examination. Because many pest control workers have access to residences and businesses, most exterminating companies require that their employees be bonded. This means an employee must be at least 18 years of age and have no criminal record.

Other Requirements

Pest control technicians should be able to use good judgment and follow oral and written instructions well. These workers should also be very conscientious and responsible, because any mistakes they make applying or handling chemicals could result in serious injury or even death for either themselves or their clients.

Pest control workers should be in good general health and able to lift fairly heavy objects. Because route workers usually make service calls alone, they need a driver's license, a safe driving record, and the ability to work well alone. Manual dexterity and mechanical ability are also important for pest control workers. Termite exterminators will also find knowledge of carpentry valuable.

EXPLORING

If you are interested in becoming a pest control worker, you might want to talk to someone already working in the field to get a good perspective on what the job is like. Students who have held part-time and summer jobs as drivers or helpers on milk, bakery, dry-cleaning, or other routes will find the experience helpful if they plan to enter this field. Also working part time in the landscaping and lawn products business would be a good experience. An interest in chemistry or, in the case of termite exterminators, in woodworking and carpentry is also an asset. More information regarding this profession can be obtained by contacting your local library or the sources at the end of this article.

EMPLOYERS

Pest control jobs are available across the country, but most of the 68,000 pest control workers in the United States are employed in large, high-density population areas. Many pest control workers are employed in states that have warmer climates. Pest control companies and landscaping and lawn services may employ pest control workers. Some government agencies and large manufacturing or processing companies may hire their own pest control workers as part of their routine maintenance. Approximately 12 percent of pest control workers operate their own businesses.

STARTING OUT

Pest control workers usually obtain their jobs through newspaper ads or leads from friends. Job seekers can also apply directly to local pest control firms listed in the Yellow Pages. Owners of firms that use the services of a pest control company may be able to provide job seekers with names of pest control firms. State and local employment offices may list job opportunities with pest control firms.

ADVANCEMENT

Skilled pest control workers may be promoted to higher paying jobs, such as route manager. Those with job experience and sales aptitude may become *pest control salespersons* who contact prospective customers to inform them of the firm's services. They might also become employees of firms that make pesticides or equipment for the industry. Other workers may get jobs as service managers and act as liaisons between the company and its customers. Some may advance to owning their own exterminating businesses. Termite exterminators who are skilled at structural work may become carpenters.

EARNINGS

Salaries vary according to geographic area, company, and job title. Beginning technicians can earn minimum wage (around $10,712 per year, depending on the state on which they work). According to the U.S. Department of Labor, the median annual earnings for all pest control workers were $27,170 in 2005. The lowest 10 percent of pest controllers earned less than $17,590, and the top 10 percent earned $43,440 or more. Some technicians receive commission based on a percentage of the service charge to the customer, and others receive a percentage of the route income.

Most pest control companies give their full-time workers regular vacations, health insurance, pension plans, and other benefits.

WORK ENVIRONMENT

Most pest control workers are employed in urban areas, where older buildings provide easy access and good shelter for roaches, rats, and other pests. Termite exterminators tend to work in suburbs and small towns, where there are many wood frame buildings. They usually work a 40-hour week, but may work longer hours in the spring and summer when insects and rodents are most active. Sometimes they have to work nights if an establishment such as a restaurant does not want spraying to occur in front of their customers.

Most pest control technicians work alone, driving to each individual client's property. They must often carry equipment and supplies weighing as much as 50 pounds. The job requires them to work both indoors and outdoors, in all kinds of weather, and they usually spend a large amount of time walking and driving. Termite exterminators may have to crawl under buildings and work in dirty or damp cellars. Therefore, people with a strong aversion to dirt and who are sensitive to unpleasant odors or who have strong allergies are not well suited to this field. In addition, because the nature of the job requires workers to spend time in pest-infested houses, anyone who is disturbed or frightened by the various bugs or rodents that might be encountered is not a good candidate.

Most of the chemicals used in exterminating are not harmful to humans if handled properly, although some may be injurious if inhaled in large quantities or left on the skin. Pest control workers wear rubber gloves when mixing the pesticides, in addition to other protective clothing. To make certain that workers are safe, some companies routinely take blood samples to test for any residual amounts of the pesticides they use.

OUTLOOK

The U.S. Department of Labor predicts that employment of pest control workers will grow faster than the average for all occupations through 2014. This growth will be due to increased environmental and health concerns, greater numbers of dual income households, and newer insulation materials that have made certain homes more susceptible to pest infestation. Although steady advances in science are resulting in safer and more effective pesticides, pest control will always be needed, since most vermin breed rapidly and develop immunity to pesticides over time. The high turnover rate among employees will also provide a certain number of job openings.

Pest control jobs are concentrated in warmer climates. Florida, Alabama, Louisiana, Arkansas, Arizona, and Hawaii have the highest concentration of pest control workers.

FOR MORE INFORMATION

*For information on education and careers in the pest control indus-
try, contact*
National Pest Management Association Inc.
9300 Lee Highway, Suite 301
Fairfax, VA 22031-6051
Tel: 703-352-6762
Email: info@pestworld.org
http://www.pestworld.org

For information on correspondence courses in pest control, contact
Purdue University
Department of Entomology
901 West State Street
West Lafayette, IN 47907-2089
Tel: 765-494-4554
http://www.entm.purdue.edu

For more information on pest control, visit
PestWorld for Kids
http://www.pestworldforkids.org

Pet Groomers

OVERVIEW

Pet groomers comb, cut, trim, and shape the fur of all types of dogs and cats. They comb out the animal's fur and trim the hair to the proper style for the size and breed. They also trim the animal's nails, bathe it, and dry its hair. In the process, they check for flea or tick infestation and any visible health problems. In order to perform these grooming tasks, the pet groomer must be able to calm the animal down and gain its confidence.

HISTORY

As long as dog has been man's best friend, humans have been striving to keep their animal companions healthy and happy. Pets are often considered members of the family and are treated as such. Just as parents take their children to the doctor for vaccinations and to the barber for haircuts, pets are often treated to regular veterinarian visits and grooming services.

An increasingly urban society and higher standards of living can both be considered significant factors in the growing number of professional grooming establishments in this country. City-dwellers who live in small apartments have less space to groom their pets than their farm-dwelling forebears had. Many busy professionals have neither the time nor the inclination to learn the proper techniques and purchase the tools needed for grooming. Additionally, many apartment and condominium buildings have regulations to which pet owners must adhere in order to ensure the safety and comfort of tenants. In compact living quarters, people don't want to encounter smelly pups in the hallway. Also, the rise of multiple-income families and an increased standard of living gives animal aficionados the disposable income to pamper their pets with professional grooming services.

Groomers are also called upon to tend to more exotic pets these days, such as ferrets, birds, and reptiles. New developments in animal grooming include high performance clippers and cutting tools, and more humane restraining devices. Current trends toward specialized services include perfuming, powdering, styling, and even massage, aromatherapy, and tattooing for pets!

THE JOB

Although all dogs and cats benefit from regular grooming, shaggy, longhaired dogs give pet groomers the bulk of their business. Some types of dogs need regular grooming for their standard appearance; among this group are poodles, schnauzers, cocker spaniels, and many types of terriers. Show dogs, or dogs that are shown in competition, are groomed frequently. Before beginning grooming, the dog groomer talks with the owner to find out the style of cut that the dog is to have. The dog groomer also relies on experience to determine how a particular breed of dog is supposed to look.

The dog groomer places the animal on a grooming table. To keep the dog steady during the clipping, a nylon collar or noose, which hangs from an adjustable pole attached to the grooming table, is slipped around its neck. The dog groomer talks to the dog or uses other techniques to keep the animal calm and gain its trust. If the dog doesn't calm down but snaps and bites instead, the groomer may have to muzzle it. If a dog is completely unmanageable, the dog groomer may ask the owner to have the dog tranquilized by a veterinarian before grooming.

After calming the dog, the groomer brushes it and tries to untangle its hair. If the dog's hair is very overgrown or is very shaggy such as an English sheepdog's, the groomer may have to cut away part of its coat with scissors before beginning any real grooming. Brushing the coat is good for both longhaired and shorthaired dogs as brushing removes shedding hair and dead skin. It also neatens the coat so the groomer can tell from the shape and proportions of the dog how to cut its hair in the most attractive way. Hair that is severely matted is actually painful to the animal because the mats pull at the animal's skin. Having these mats removed is necessary to the animal's health and comfort.

Once the dog is brushed, the groomer cuts and shapes the dog's coat with electric clippers. Next, the dog's ears are cleaned and its nails are trimmed. The groomer must take care not to cut the nails too short because they may bleed and cause the dog pain. If the nails do bleed, a special powder is applied to stop the bleeding. The comfort of the animal is an important concern for the groomer.

The dog is then given a bath, sometimes by a worker known as a *dog bather*. The dog is lowered into a stainless steel tub, sprayed with warm water, scrubbed with a special shampoo, and rinsed. This may be repeated several times if the dog is very dirty. The dog groomer has special chemicals that can be used to deodorize a dog that has encountered a skunk or has gone for a swim in foul water. If a dog has fleas or ticks, the dog groomer treats them at this stage by soaking the wet coat with a solution to kill the insects. This toxic solution must be kept out of the dog's eyes, ears, and nose, which may be cleaned more carefully with a sponge or washcloth. A hot oil treatment may also be applied to condition the dog's coat.

The groomer dries the dog after bathing, either with a towel, hand-held electric blower, or in a drier cage with electric blow driers. Poodles and some other types of dogs have their coats fluff-dried, then scissored for the final pattern or style. Poodles, which at one time were the mainstay of the dog grooming business, generally take the longest to groom because of their intricate clipping pattern. Most dogs can be groomed in about 90 minutes, although grooming may

Professional groomers prepare to brush a dog. *(Grantpix/Index Stock Imagery)*

Facts About Pets

- Approximately 63 percent of people in the United States own a pet—an increase of 7 percent since 1988.
- Forty-five percent of U.S. households have more than one pet.
- In 2005, U.S. consumers spent $36.3 billion on pets and pet care.
- Medical studies have shown that pets help lower blood pressure, reduce stress, fight depression, prevent heart disease, and otherwise improve the health of their owners.

Source: American Pet Products Manufacturers Association

take several hours for shaggier breeds whose coats are badly matted and overgrown.

More and more cats, especially longhaired breeds, are now being taken to pet groomers. The procedure for cats is the same as for dogs, although cats are not dipped when bathed. As the dog or cat is groomed, the groomer checks to be sure there are no signs of disease in the animal's eyes, ears, skin, or coat. If there are any abnormalities, such as bald patches or skin lesions, the groomer tells the owner and may recommend that a veterinarian check the animal. The groomer may also give the owner tips on animal hygiene.

Pet owners and those in pet care generally have respect for pet groomers who do a good job and treat animals well. Many people, especially those who raise show dogs, grow to rely on particular pet groomers to do a perfect job each time. Pet groomers can earn satisfaction from taking a shaggy, unkempt animal and transforming it into a beautiful creature. On the other hand, some owners may unfairly blame the groomer if the animal becomes ill while in the groomer's care, or for some malady or condition that is not the groomer's fault.

Because they deal with both the pets and their owners, pet groomers can find their work both challenging and rewarding. One owner of a grooming business asserts, "Nothing feels better than developing a relationship with pets and their owners. It's almost like they become an extended part of the family. When working with living animals you accept the responsibility of caring for them to the best of your ability, and the rewards are great. I don't think that can be said of a mechanic or furnace repairman."

REQUIREMENTS

High School

A high school diploma generally is not required for people working as pet groomers. A diploma or GED certificate, however, can be a great asset to people who would like to advance within their present company or move to other careers in animal care that require more training, such as veterinary technicians. Useful courses include English, business math, general science, anatomy and physiology, health, zoology, psychology, bookkeeping, office management, typing, art, and first aid.

Postsecondary Training

A person interested in pet grooming can be trained for the field in one of three ways: enrolling in a pet grooming school; working in a pet shop or kennel and learning on the job; or reading one of the many books on pet grooming and practicing on his or her own pet.

To enroll in most pet grooming schools, a person must be at least 17 years old and fond of animals. Previous experience in pet grooming can sometimes be applied for course credits. Students study a wide range of topics including the basics of bathing, brushing, and clipping; the care of ears and nails; coat and skin conditions; animal anatomy terminology; and sanitation. They also study customer relations, which is very important for those who plan to operate their own shops. During training, students practice their techniques on actual animals, which people bring in for grooming at a discount rate. You can access a list of pet grooming schools by visiting http://www.petgroomer.com. Many other grooming schools advertise in dog and pet magazines. It is important for students to choose an accredited, state-licensed school in order to increase both their employment opportunities and professional knowledge.

Students can also learn pet grooming while working for a grooming shop, kennel, animal hospital, or veterinarian's office. They usually begin with tasks such as shampooing dogs and cats, and trimming their nails, then gradually work their way up to brushing and basic haircuts. With experience, they may learn more difficult cuts and use these skills to earn more pay or start their own business.

The essentials of pet grooming can also be learned from the many books available on the subject. These books are often species or breed specific, so plan on reading more than one. A good guide will contain all the information a person needs to know to start his or her own pet grooming business, including the basic cuts, bathing and handling techniques, and type of equipment needed. Still, many of the finer points of grooming, such as the more complicated cuts and various safety precautions, are best learned while working under an experienced groomer. There still is no substitute for on-the-job training and experience.

Certification or Licensing
Presently, state licensing or certification is not required, and there are no established labor unions for pet groomers. To start a grooming salon or other business, a license is needed from the city or town in which a person plans to practice. The National Dog Groomers Association of America (NDGAA) offers certification to groomers who pass written and practical examinations.

Other Requirements
The primary qualification for a person who wants to work with pets is a love of animals. Animals can sense when someone does not like them or is afraid of them. A person needs certain skills in order to work with nervous, aggressive, or fidgety animals. They must be patient with the animals, able to gain their respect, and enjoy giving the animals a lot of love and attention. Persistence and endurance are also helpful, as grooming one animal can take several hours of strenuous work. Groomers should enjoy working with their hands and have good eyesight and manual dexterity to accurately cut a clipping pattern.

EXPLORING

To find out if you are suited for a job in pet grooming, you should familiarize yourself with animals as much as possible. This can be done in many ways, starting with the proper care of your dog, cat, or other family pet. You can also offer to tend to the pets of friends and neighbors to see how well you handle unfamiliar animals. Youth organizations such as the Boy Scouts, Girl Scouts, and 4-H Clubs sponsor projects that give members the chance to raise and care for animals. You can also volunteer or work part time caring for animals at an animal hospital, kennel, pet shop, animal shelter, nature center, or zoo.

EMPLOYERS

Grooming salons, kennels, pet shops, veterinary practices, animal hospitals, and grooming schools employ pet groomers. The pet business is thriving all over the country, and the opportunities for groomers are expected to increase steadily in the coming years. Although most employers can offer attractive benefits packages, many pet groomers choose to go into business for themselves rather than turn over 40 to 50 percent of their fees to their employers. Graduates of accredited pet grooming schools benefit from the schools' job placement services, which can help students find work in the kind of setting they prefer.

STARTING OUT

Graduates from dog grooming schools can take advantage of the schools' job placement services. Generally, there are more job openings than qualified groomers to fill them, so new graduates may have several job offers to consider. These schools learn of job openings in all parts of the United States and are usually happy to contact prospective employers and write letters of introduction for graduates.

The NDGAA also promotes professional identification through membership and certification testing throughout the United States and Canada. The NDGAA offers continuing education, accredited workshops, certification testing, seminars, insurance programs, a job placement program, membership directory, and other services and products. Other associations of interest to dog groomers are the Humane Society of the United States and the United Kennel Club. Because dog groomers are concerned with the health and safety of the animals they service, membership in groups that promote and protect animal welfare is very common.

Other sources of job information include the classified ads of daily newspapers and listings in dog and pet magazines. Job leads may be available from private or state employment agencies or from referrals of salon or kennel owners. People looking for work should phone or send letters to prospective employers, inform them of their qualifications, and, if invited, visit their establishments.

ADVANCEMENT

Pet groomers who work for other people may advance to a more responsible position such as office manager or dog trainer. If dog groomers start their own shops, they may become successful enough to expand or to open branch offices or area franchises. Skilled groomers may want to work for a dog grooming school as an instructor, possibly advancing to a job as a school director, placement officer, or other type of administrator.

The pet industry is booming, so there are many avenues of advancement for groomers who like to work with pets. With more education, a groomer may get a job as a veterinary technician or assistant at a shelter or animal hospital. Those who like to train dogs may open obedience schools, train guide dogs, work with field and hunting dogs, or even train stunt and movie dogs. People can also open their own kennels, breeding and pedigree services, gaming dog businesses, or pet supply distribution firms. Each of these requires specialized knowledge and experience, so additional study, education, and work is often needed.

EARNINGS

Groomers charge either by the job or the hour. If they are on the staff of a salon or work for another groomer, they get to keep 50 to 60 percent of the fees they charge. For this reason, many groomers branch off to start their own businesses. "I would never want to go back to working for someone else or giving up a commission on my groomings," says one owner-operator of a grooming business.

The U.S. Department of Labor reports that median hourly earnings of nonfarm animal caretakers (the category in which pet groomers are classified) were $8.52 (or $17,720 annually) in 2005. Salaries ranged from less than $6.43 (or $13,380 annually) to more than $14.85 per hour (or $30,890 annually). Those who own and operate their own grooming services can earn significantly more, depending on how hard they work, the clientele they service, and the economy of the area in which they work.

Groomers generally buy their own clipping equipment, including barber's shears, brushes, and clippers. A new set of equipment costs around $325; used sets cost less. Groomers employed full time at salons, grooming schools, pet shops, animal hospitals, and kennels often get a full range of benefits, including paid vacations and holidays, medical and dental insurance, and retirement pensions.

WORK ENVIRONMENT

Salons, kennels, and pet shops, as well as gaming and breeding services, should be clean and well lighted, with modern equipment and clean surroundings. Establishments that do not meet these standards endanger the health of the animals that are taken there, and the owners of these establishments should be reported. Groomers who are self-employed may work out of their homes. Some groomers buy vans and convert them into grooming shops. They drive them to the homes of the pets they work on, which many owners find very convenient. Those who operate these "groommobiles" may work on 30 or 40 dogs a week, and factor their driving time and expenses into their fees.

Groomers usually work a 40-hour week and may have to work evenings or weekends. Those who own their own shops or work out of their homes, like other self-employed people, work very long hours and may have irregular schedules. One groomer points out that, "You can't just decide to call in sick when you have seven dogs scheduled to be groomed that day. We have had midnight emergency calls from clients needing immediate help of one kind or another with their pet." Many groomers/business owners believe that the occasionally hectic schedule of the field is not always a negative aspect, since they take great pride in being able to offer personal service and care to both animals and clients.

Groomers are on their feet much of the day, and their work can get very tiring when they have to lift and restrain large animals. They must wear comfortable clothing that allows for freedom of movement, but they should also be presentable enough to deal with pet owners and other clients.

When working with any sort of animal, a person may encounter bites, scratches, strong odors, fleas, and other insects. They may have to deal with sick or bad-tempered animals. The groomer must regard every animal as a unique individual and treat it with respect. Groomers need to be careful while on the job, especially when handling flea and tick killers, which are toxic to humans as well as to pests.

OUTLOOK

The demand for skilled dog groomers has grown faster than average, and is expected to continue to grow at this rate through 2014, according to the U.S. Department of Labor. Every year more people are keeping dogs and cats as pets. They are spending more money to pamper their animals, but often don't have enough free time or the inclination to groom their pets themselves. Grooming is not just a luxury for pets, however, because regular attention makes it more likely that any injury or illness will be noticed and treated.

Also, as nontraditional pets become more mainstream, innovative groomers will need to take advantage of new techniques and facilities for bringing animals other than dogs and cats into the pet salon.

FOR MORE INFORMATION

For more information about grooming and related professions including grooming competitions and conferences, contact
Intergroom
76 Carol Drive
Dedham, MA 02026-6635
Tel: 781-326-3376
http://www.intergroom.com

For information on shows, new grooming products and techniques, and workshop and certification test sites and dates, contact
National Dog Groomers Association of America Inc.
PO Box 101
Clark, PA 16113-0101
Tel: 724-962-2711
Email: ndga@nationaldoggroomers.com
http://www.nationaldoggroomers.com

For information on pet grooming schools, contact the following institutions
California School of Dog Grooming
655 South Rancho Santa Fe Road
San Marcos, CA 92069-3973
Tel: 800-949-3746
Email: gtaurasi@csdg.net
http://www.csdg.net

Nash Academy of Animal Arts (Kentucky)
857 Lane Allen Road
Lexington, KY 40504-3605
Tel: 859-277-2763
Email: info@nashacademy.com
http://www.nashacademy.com

Nash Academy of Animal Arts (New Jersey)
653 Anderson Avenue
Cliffside Park, NJ 07010-1920
Tel: 201-945-2710
Email: info@nashacademy.co
http://www.nashacademy.com

New York School of Dog Grooming
455 Second Avenue
New York, NY 10010-2403

Tel: 212-685-3776 or 800-541-5541
Email: nysdg@nysdg.com
http://www.nysdg.com

For links to additional pet grooming career information, visit
PetGroomer.com
http://www.petgroomer.com

Pet Sitters

QUICK FACTS

School Subjects
Business
Family and consumer science

Personal Skills
Following instructions
Helping/teaching

Work Environment
Indoors and outdoors
Primarily multiple locations

Minimum Education Level
High school diploma

Salary Range
$5,000 to $20,000 to
$100,000+

Certification or Licensing
Voluntary

Outlook
Faster than the average

DOT
N/A

GOE
N/A

NOC
0651, 6483

O*NET-SOC
39-2021.00

OVERVIEW

When pet owners are on vacation or working long hours, they hire *pet sitters* to come to their homes and visit their animals. During short, daily visits, pet sitters feed the animals, play with them, clean up after them, give them medications when needed, and let them in and out of the house for exercise. *Dog walkers* may be responsible only for taking their clients' pets out for exercise. Pet sitters may also be available for overnight stays, looking after the houses of clients as well as their pets.

HISTORY

Animals have been revered by humans for centuries, as is evidenced by early drawings on the walls of caves and tombs—cats were even considered sacred by the ancient Egyptians. Though these sacred cats may have had their own personal caretakers, it has only been within the last 10 years that pet sitting has evolved into a successful industry and a viable career option. Before groups such as the National Association of Professional Pet Sitters (NAPPS), which formed in the early 1980s, and Pet Sitters International (PSI) were developed, pet sitting was regarded as a way for people with spare time to make a little extra money on the side. Like babysitting, pet sitting attracted primarily teenagers and women; many children's books over the last century have depicted the trials and tribulations of young entrepreneurs in the business of pet sitting and dog walking. Patti Moran, the founder of both NAPPS and PSI, and author of *Pet Sitting for Profit*, is credited with helping pet sitters gain recognition as successful small business owners. Though many people still only pet sit occasionally for neighbors and friends, others are developing long lists of clientele and proving strong competition to kennels and boarding facilities.

THE JOB

If you live in a big city, you've seen them hit the streets with their packs of dogs. Dragged along by four or five leashes, the pet sitter walks the dogs down the busy sidewalks, allowing the animals their afternoon exercise while the pet owners are stuck in the office. You may not have realized it, but those dog walkers are probably the owners of thriving businesses. Though a hobby for some, pet sitting is for others a demanding career with many responsibilities. Michele Finley is one of these pet sitters, in the Park Slope neighborhood of Brooklyn, New York. "A lot of people seem to think pet sitting is a walk in the park (pun intended)," she says, "and go into it without realizing what it entails (again)."

For those who can't bear to leave their dogs or cats at kennels or boarders while they are away, pet sitters offer peace of mind to the owners, as well as their pets. With a pet sitter, pets can stay in familiar surroundings, as well as avoid the risks of illnesses passed on by other animals. The pets are also assured routine exercise and no disruptions in their diets. Most pet sitters prefer to work only with cats and dogs, but pet sitters are also called upon to care for birds, reptiles, gerbils, fish, and other animals.

With their own set of keys, pet sitters let themselves into the homes of their clients and care for their animals while they're away at work or on vacation. Pet sitters feed the animals, make sure they have water, and give them their medications. They clean up any messes the animals have made and clean litter boxes. They give the animals attention, playing with them, letting them outside, and taking them for walks. Usually, a pet sitter can provide pet owners with a variety of personal pet care services—they may take a pet to the vet, offer grooming, sell pet-related products, and give advice. Some pet sitters take dogs out into the country, to mountain parks, or to lakes, for exercise in wide-open spaces. "You should learn to handle each pet as an individual," Finley advises. "Just because Fluffy likes his ears scratched doesn't mean Spot does."

Pet sitters typically plan one to three visits (of 30 to 60 minutes in length) per day, or they may make arrangements to spend the night. In addition to caring for the animals, pet sitters also look after the houses of their clients. They bring in the newspapers and the mail; they water the plants; they make sure the house is securely locked.

The Most Popular Pets

Number of U.S. Households That Own a Pet

Dog	43.5 million
Cat	37.7 million
Freshwater Fish	13.9 million
Bird	6.4 million
Small Animal	5.7 million
Reptile	4.4 million
Equine	4.2 million

Source: American Pet Products Manufacturers Association

Pet sitters generally charge by the hour or per visit. They may also have special pricing for overtime, emergency situations, extra duties, and travel.

Most pet sitters work alone, without employees, no matter how demanding the work. Though this means they get to keep all the money, it also means they keep all the responsibilities. A successful pet-sitting service requires a fair amount of business management. Finley works directly with the animals from 10:00 A.M. until 5:00 or 6:00 P.M., with no breaks; upon returning home, she will have five to 10 phone messages from clients. Part of her evening then consists of scheduling and rescheduling appointments, offering advice on feeding, training, and other pet care concerns, and giving referrals for boarders and vets. But despite these hours, and despite having to work holidays, as well as days when she's not feeling well, Finley appreciates many things about the job. "Being with the furries all day is the best," she says. She also likes not having to dress up for work and not having to commute to an office.

REQUIREMENTS

High School
As a pet sitter, you'll be running your own business all by yourself; therefore you should take high school courses such as accounting, marketing, and office skills. Computer science will help you learn about the software you'll need for managing accounts and schedul-

ing. Join a school business group that will introduce you to business practices and local entrepreneurs.

Science courses such as biology and chemistry, as well as health courses, will give you some good background for developing animal care skills. As a pet sitter, you'll be overseeing the health of the animals, their exercise, and their diets. You'll also be preparing medications and administering eye and ear drops.

As a high school student, you can easily gain hands-on experience as a pet sitter. If you know anyone in your neighborhood with pets, volunteer to care for the animals whenever the owners go on vacation. Once you've got experience and a list of references, you may even be able to start a part-time job for yourself as a pet sitter.

Postsecondary Training

Many pet sitters start their own businesses after having gained experience in other areas of animal care. Vet techs and pet shop workers may promote their animal care skills to develop a clientele for more profitable pet-sitting careers. Graduates from a business college may recognize pet sitting as a great way to start a business with little overhead. But neither a vet tech qualification nor a business degree is required to become a successful pet sitter. And the only special training you need to pursue is actual experience. A local pet shop or chapter of the ASPCA may offer seminars in various aspects of animal care; the NAPPS offers a mentorship program, as well as a newsletter, while PSI sponsors correspondence programs.

Certification or Licensing

PSI offers the accredited pet sitter designation to applicants who pass an open book examination that covers topics in four major categories: pet care, health and nutrition, business and office procedures, and additional services. Accreditation must be renewed every three years. The National Association of Professional Pet Sitters offers the certified pet sitter designation to applicants who complete a home-study course and pass an examination.

Michele Finley has a different view on certification. "I really don't think such things are necessary," she says. "All you need to know can be learned by working for a good sitter and reading pet health and behavioral newsletters."

Though there is no particular pet-sitting license required of pet sitters, insurance protection is important. Liability insurance protects the pet sitter from lawsuits; both NAPPS and PSI offer group liability packages to its members. Pet sitters must also be bonded. Bonding assures the pet owners that if anything is missing from their homes after a pet sitting appointment, they can receive compensation immediately.

Other Requirements

You must love animals and animals must love you. But this love for animals can't be your only motivation—keep in mind that, as a pet sitter, you'll be in business for yourself. You won't have a boss to give you assignments, and you won't have a secretary or bookkeeper to do the paperwork. You also won't have employees to take over on weekends, holidays, and days when you're not feeling well. Though some pet sitters are successful enough to afford assistance, most must handle all the aspects of their businesses by themselves. So, you should be self-motivated and as dedicated to the management of your business as you are to the animals.

Pet owners entrust you with the care of their pets and their homes, so you must be trustworthy and reliable. You should also be organized and prepared for emergency situations. And not only must you be patient with the pets and their owners, but also with the development of your business: it will take a few years to build up a good list of clients.

As a pet sitter, you must also be ready for the dirty work—you'll be cleaning litter boxes and animal messes within the house. On dog walks, you'll be picking up after them on the street. You may be giving animals medications. You'll also be cleaning aquariums and birdcages.

"Work for an established pet sitter to see how you like it," Finley advises. "It's a very physically demanding job and not many can stand it for long on a full-time basis." Pet sitting isn't for those who just want a nine-to-five desk job. Your day will be spent moving from house to house, taking animals into back-yards, and walking dogs around the neighborhoods. Though you may be able to develop a set schedule for yourself, you really will have to arrange your work hours around the hours of your clients. Some pet sitters start in the early morning hours, while others only work afternoons or evenings. To stay in business, a pet sitter must be prepared to work weekends, holidays, and long hours in the summertime.

EXPLORING

There are many books, newsletters, and magazines devoted to pet care. *Pet Sitting for Profit: A Complete Manual for Professional Success* (Howell Book House, 1997), by Patti Moran, is just one of many books that can offer insight into pet sitting as a career. Magazines such as *The WORLD of Professional Pet Sitting* (http://www.petsit.com/pubs.asp) can also teach you

Pet sitters must be in excellent shape in order to be able to manage large numbers of animals at one time. *(John Dominis, Index Stock Imagery)*

about the requirements of professional animal care. And there are countless books discussing the ins and outs of small business ownership.

Try pet sitting for a neighbor or family member to get a sense of the responsibilities of the job. Some pet sitters hire assistants on an independent contractor basis; contact an area pet sitter who is listed in the phone book or with one of the professional organizations, and see if you can "hire on" for a day or two. Not only will you learn firsthand the duties of a pet sitter, but you'll also see how the business is run.

EMPLOYERS

Nearly all pet sitters are self-employed, although a few may work for other successful pet sitters who have built up a large enough clientele to require help. It takes most pet sitters an appreciable period of time to build up a business substantial enough to make a living without other means of income. The outlook for this field is excellent, however, and start-up costs are minimal, making it a good choice for animal lovers who want to work for themselves. For those who have good business sense and a great deal of ambition, the potential for success is strong.

STARTING OUT

You're not likely to find job listings under "pet sitter" in the news-paper. Most pet sitters schedule all their work themselves, but you may find ads in the classifieds or in weekly community papers, from pet owners looking to hire pet sitters. Some people who become pet sitters have backgrounds in animal care—they may have worked for vets, breeders, or pet shops. These people enter the business with a client list already in hand, having made contacts with many pet owners. But, if you're just starting out in animal care, you need to develop a list of references. This may mean volunteering your time to friends and neighbors, or working very cheaply. If you're willing to actually stay in the house while the pet owners are on vacation, you should be able to find plenty of pet-sitting opportunities in the summertime. Post your name, phone number, and availability on the bulletin boards of grocery stores, colleges, and coffee shops around town. Once you've developed a list of references, and have made connections with pet owners, you can start expanding, and increasing your profits.

Susan Clark runs a professional dog-walking business in Brooklyn, New York. She suggests another way of breaking into the business. "I started my business," she says, "by visiting pet stores and asking if they would supply me with their mailing lists; in return, when I went door to door with my own postcards, I would include their business cards. Many pet store owners were kind enough to agree to this arrangement. I have to say, though, the majority of my business came from two other sources: word of mouth and referrals from other dog walkers in the neighborhood. I knew a great deal of dog owners in the area because I would go to the dog runs with my own two dogs. The minute I mentioned I was thinking about opening up a dog-walking service, I was in business. My dog walker and boarder were incredibly supportive and also sent business my way. I was very fortunate, and have never forgotten their generosity, so I do the same for other new dog walkers in the neighborhood."

ADVANCEMENT

Your advancement will be a result of your own hard work; the more time you dedicate to your business, the bigger the business will become. The success of any small business can be very unpredict-able. For some, a business can build very quickly, for others, it may take years. Some pet sitters start out part time, perhaps even volunteering, then may find themselves with enough business to quit their full-time jobs and devote themselves entirely to pet sitting. Once your business takes off, you may be able to afford an assistant, or an entire staff. Some pet sitters even have franchises across the country. You may even choose to develop your business into a much larger operation, such as a dog day care facility.

EARNINGS

Pet sitters set their own prices, charging by the visit, the hour, or the week. They may also charge consultation fees, and additional fees on holidays. They may have special pricing plans in place, such as for emergency situations or for administering medications. Depending on the kinds of animals (sometimes pet sitters charge less to care for cats than dogs), pet sitters generally charge between $8 and $15 for a 30-minute visit. The average per-visit rate is $13.20, according to Pet Sitters International (PSI). PSI conducted a recent survey of annual salaries and discovered that the range was too great to determine a median. Some very successful pet sitters have annual salaries of more than $100,000, while others only make $5,000 a year. Though a pet sitter can make a good profit in any area of the country, a bigger city will offer more clients. Pet sitters in their first five years of business are unlikely to make more than $10,000 a year; pet sitters who have had businesses for eight years or more may make more than $40,000 a year.

WORK ENVIRONMENT

Some pet sitters prefer to work close to their homes; Michele Finley only walks dogs in her Brooklyn neighborhood. In a smaller town, however, pet sitters have to do a fair amount of driving from place to place. Depending on the needs of the animals, the pet sitter will let the pets outside for play and exercise. Although filling food and water bowls and performing other chores within the house is generally peaceful work, walking dogs on busy city sidewalks can be stressful. And in the wintertime, you'll spend a fair amount of time out in the inclement weather. "Icy streets are murder," Finley says. "And I don't like dealing with people who hate dogs and are always yelling to get the dog away from them."

Though you'll have some initial interaction with pet owners when getting house keys, taking down phone numbers, and meeting the pets and learning about their needs, most of your work will be alone with the animals. But you won't be totally isolated; if dog walking in the city, you'll meet other dog owners and other people in the neighborhood.

OUTLOOK

Pet sitting as a small business is expected to skyrocket in the coming years. Most pet sitters charge fees comparable to kennels and boarders, but some charge less. And many pet owners prefer to leave their pets in the house, rather than take the pets to unfamiliar locations. This has made pet sitting a desirable and cost-effective alternative to other pet care situations. Pet sitters have been successful in cities both large and small. In the last few years, pet sitting has been featured in the *Wall Street Journal* and other national publications. *Woman's Day* magazine listed pet sitting as one of the top-grossing businesses for women.

Because a pet sitting business requires little money to start up, many more people may enter the business hoping to make a tidy profit. This could lead to heavier competition; it could also hurt the reputation of pet sitting if too many irresponsible and unprepared people run bad businesses. But if pet owners remain cautious when hiring pet sitters, the unreliable workers will have trouble maintaining clients.

FOR MORE INFORMATION

For information about pet care, contact
American Society for the Prevention of Cruelty to Animals
424 East 92nd Street
New York, NY 10128-6804
Tel: 212-876-7700
http://www.aspca.org

For information on pet setting and certification, contact
National Association of Professional Pet Sitters
15000 Commerce Parkway, Suite C
Mt. Laurel, NJ 08054-2212
Tel: 856-439-0324
Email: napps@ahint.com
http://www.petsitters.org

For certification, careers, and small business information, as well as general information about pet sitting, contact

Pet Sitters International
201 East King Street
King, NC 27021-9161
Tel: 336-983-9222
Email: info@petsit.com
http://www.petsit.com

───── INTERVIEW ─────

Jerry Wentz is the owner of Homesitters of Raleigh, a pet sitting business in Raleigh, North Carolina. He is also the president of the National Association of Professional Pet Sitters. Jerry discussed his career with the editors of Careers in Focus: Personal Services.

Q. Please tell us about your work as a petsitting business owner.

A. I bought the business from a previous owner in 1990. I had previously been a restaurant manager, and graduated from East Carolina University in 1980 with a Bachelor of Science degree in business administration. My work consists mostly of managing my employees and interacting with potential and actual customers. I do very little pet sitting now, although I did quite a bit when we were new in the business. Recruiting, screening, hiring, training, and working with my 20 part-time employees is a big part of what I do. I am also responsible for marketing/advertising, payroll, customer service—all administrative aspects of the business.

Q. What are the most important personal and professional qualities for people in your career?

A. As a pet sitter: the same attributes as in any service position are required, plus you must love and be knowledgeable about animals. A passion for whatever you do is one of the key ingredients to success. The service field is about customers trading money to have a problem solved—in this case, that they will be away and need care for their pets. Many people assume that, in this business, one needs to be concerned mainly with being able to get along with animals, but every customer-service person in this type of business, or any other, should be able to make their customers feel as though they are valued for the job they provide, and that the employee's and business' reason for being is to serve them in a manner that recognizes that fact, and also the employee's commitment to effectively solving their problem.

As an owner/manager: the same [attributes] as in any other management position, plus loving and being knowledgeable about animals. The ability to communicate effectively, professionally, and politely is very important. Leadership skills require the commitment to communicate company values to employees and customers, set an example that places those values in high regard, and motivate others to follow. It is also important to be able to communicate the key factors that differentiate your business from the competition and persuade potential customers that you can meet their needs. Problem resolution occasionally comes into play also.

Q. What activities would you suggest to high school students who are interested in this career?

A. Find an employer in the animal field that you observe to be a professional at customer service. Work for them and ask them to help mentor you (most people love to share their knowledge) in developing the skills to deal with the many unusual things that can happen in customer service.

Q. What are some of the pros and cons of your job?

A. Pros: Working with animals is a big factor for many people. Animal lovers tend to be nice folks, so we work with really nice people, too, both employees and customers. As the business owner, I usually have a lot of flexibility to decide my own schedule. This is very important to me since I have two teenagers.

Cons: Holidays are busy. Rarely, but on occasion, there are customers who can be difficult to satisfy. This is true in any service position, but less true in this field. Again, animal lovers tend to be nice people.

Q. What is the future employment outlook for pet sitters? Is this a growing field?

A. Working for someone else as a pet sitter is usually more of a part-time or hourly position. More money and opportunity exist for personal and professional growth in owning your own business, and having others work for you. According to the American Pet Products Manufacturers Association, the cottage industry of pet sitting has only reached a 3 percent market penetration nationwide, so the growth potential is enormous.

Spa Attendants

OVERVIEW

Spa attendants work in hotels, resorts, and salons. They are specially trained in facial, body, and water treatments. They assist massage therapists and estheticians, and prepare and clean the treatment rooms and tables. They provide spa customers with refreshments, towels, washcloths, and robes. According to the International SPA Association, there are 280,700 people employed by the more than 12,100 spas in the United States.

HISTORY

Fossils prove that even the mammoths of over 20,000 years ago enjoyed a good spa treatment. The town of Hot Springs, a small resort village nestled in the hills of South Dakota, features a fossil excavation site; this site serves as evidence that mammoths were attracted to the area's pools of warm water. Humans share this attraction. Native Americans considered natural hot springs to be sacred healing grounds. All through Europe, the ancient Romans built colossal spas, including the Baths of Caracalla, one of the seven wonders of the world. Only its ruins remain, but Caracalla once featured hot and cold baths, a swimming pool, a gymnasium, shops, art galleries, and acres of gardens.

Although spas fell out of favor during the Middle Ages, by the 17th and 18th centuries, they had once again become popular in Europe. An interest in making use of natural resources for healing and relaxation spread, and by the late 1800s, there was hardly a well of natural spring water in the United States that a businessman hadn't capitalized upon. At the turn of the century in the United

QUICK FACTS

School Subjects
Chemistry
Health

Personal Skills
Communication/ideas
Helping/teaching

Work Environment
Primarily indoors
Primarily one location

Minimum Education Level
High school diploma

Salary Range
$12,000 to $21,000 to
$30,000

Certification or Licensing
None available

Outlook
About as fast as the average

DOT
N/A

GOE
N/A

NOC
N/A

O*NET-SOC
N/A

States, people visited resorts and spas (with or without natural hot springs) for exercise and relaxation. By the 1920s, spas had become popular retreats for the wealthy. Since that time, spas have diversified their services and attracted a wide range of visitors. Today's spas have clients ranging from busy professionals looking for several hours of stress reduction, to families looking for healthy vacations, to pregnant women seeking relaxation, to men looking to keep fit. According to the International SPA Association, there were approximately 136 million spa visits in the United States in 2003.

THE JOB

From the ylang ylang plant to the lomilomi massage, spa attendants are teaching vacationers a new language of health and rejuvenation. Although there were only 30 spas in the United States in the late 1970s, the number now has grown past 12,000. More than 70 percent of these are day spas, where clients can check in for an afternoon of relaxation and rejuvenation. The remainder are resort/hotel spas, which welcome clients for longer visits. Spas and resorts have cropped up around natural hot springs, the seaside, the desert, the mountains, and even the plains. Some spas are designed to meet very specific needs, such as weight management and holistic wellness. While most spas offer the usual facials, body wraps, and massages, many are expanding to include "mind/body awareness" as people flock to spas for both physical and spiritual needs. In some spas, you can schedule hypnosis, yoga, and dream therapy sessions right after your horseback riding, tennis game, and round of golf. So the duties of a spa attendant can vary greatly from location to location. Spa attendants are also finding work outside of the vacation industry, at salons and day spas, as cosmetologists recognize the need to expand into other areas of beauty care. In addition to actually performing treatments, spa attendants devise special treatment plans for individual clients. They also schedule appointments, order and sell products, launder linens, and clean all spa areas. They offer advice on treatments and skin care products.

Craig Rabago works as a men's spa technician for the Ihilani Resort and Spa in Kapolei, Hawaii. *Ihilani* means "heavenly splendor," and it is part of Rabago's job to help guests realize this splendor. "I create an atmosphere that is heavenly for them," Rabago explains. "I'm of Hawaiian descent and a local. I give people a warm welcome and make them feel at home." Rabago has been trained in a variety of services, including seaweed wraps, salt scrubs, and thalasso hydrotherapy (a fresh seawater massage). The Ihilani features a fitness center and separate spas for men and women; each spa includes a sauna, steam room, needle shower, hot tub, and cold plunge. For the popular "cool ti leaf wrap," Rabago prepares a table in one of the spa's private rooms, spreading out the long, frond-like Hawaiian ti leaves and treating them with special oils. When the guest arrives for his wrap, Rabago gives him a robe and sandals and shows him to the lockers and then the showers. When the guest is ready for the treatment, Rabago then brings him to the treatment room and directs him to lie back on the table. As he explains the treatment, Rabago rubs the guest's skin with oils and lotions, making sure to pay special attention to sunburn, dry skin, and other trouble areas. He then wraps the guest in a damp sheet. Rabago leaves him wrapped for 25 minutes, checking in occasionally to make sure the guest is comfortable. In between treatments, Rabago must take linen inventory and keep the spa areas clean. He also does a fair amount of work on the computer. "But taking care of the guests' needs—that's my priority," Rabago says.

The Ihilani capitalizes on its locale, providing treatments with fresh seawater, sea salt, seaweed, and Hawaiian plants. In a different kind of environment, a spa and resort may provide very different services. Mud baths, natural hot spring whirlpools, volcanic mineral treatment—resort owners around the world develop their spas with the natural surroundings in mind. This results in very specific training for spa attendants. "The training was time-consuming," Rabago recalls. "The spa techs train with each other. We put in lots of hours of practice before we actually go to work on a guest."

REQUIREMENTS

High School

To prepare for work as a spa attendant, take high school courses in anatomy, physiology, and biology. These classes will give you an understanding of the human body and muscle systems. Chemistry will prepare you for the use and preparation of skin care products. Health courses will teach you about nutrition, fitness, and other issues of importance to the health-conscious patrons of resorts and spas. Because so many spas offer treatment for both the body and the mind, take some psychology courses to learn about the history of treating depression, anxiety, and other mental and emotional problems. Finally, take computer classes, which will allow you to become comfortable using this technology. If in your future job you need to keep track of spa supplies, you will probably be using a computer to do so.

In addition to these classes, you will benefit from having CPR and first-aid training. Check with your high school to find out if it offers such training or contact organizations such as your local Red Cross. Many spas require attendants to know CPR and first aid, and your training will give you an advantage when looking for a job. Currently no specific postsecondary training program exists for spa attendants. Most spas put new hires through their own attendant-training programs. Any work experience that you already have in a spa, therefore, will make you an appealing job candidate. During your high school years, try to get a summer job at one of the many resorts across the country. Spas often hire extra help to deal with the increased number of guests during this peak vacation period. Although you may only be working with the laundry, you will have the opportunity to see how a spa or resort is run and find out about the many different jobs available.

Some spas require their attendants to be certified cosmeticians or massage therapists. In such cases, education beyond high school is required. If you know of a specific spa at which you wish to work, ask about the hiring policy for attendants. Cosmeticians receive their training from cosmetology schools; massage therapists are educated at schools of massage therapy. Licensing requirements for these professionals vary by state, and you should know what these requirements are before you begin a program of study.

Other Requirements

Craig Rabago of the Ihilani advises that a good spa attendant should "be happy, courageous, and ambitious." Guests of resorts and spas expect to be pampered and welcomed and can only fully relax during a spa treatment if the attendant is calm and considerate. Be prepared to serve your clients and to remain friendly and helpful. "But don't be timid and shy," Rabago says. "This is a good way to meet people from all around the world. You can broaden your horizons."

Any shyness and excessive modesty may also prevent you from performing your spa duties properly. You'll be applying lotions and oils to the naked skin of your guests—if you are uncomfortable, your clients will detect it and become uncomfortable themselves. You must take a professional approach so that your clients feel safe and at ease. You should have a good "bedside manner"—the calm, comforting approach health care professionals use. Self-confidence is also important; you must convey to your client that you're knowledgeable about the treatment.

EXPLORING

One of the best ways to explore this type of work is to get a part-time or summer job at a spa. You may be surprised by the number of spas in your area. There may even be a resort on the outskirts of your city. Look in the Yellow Pages under "Beauty Salons and Services" as well as "Health Clubs" and "Massage." (Many of the listings under "Spa" are only for hot tub dealerships.) Visit a salon or day spa and ask to interview someone who works as a spa attendant. Some attendants may allow you to shadow them for a day or two. Larger salons may have openings for part-time attendants, allowing you to gather firsthand experience.

Many resorts across the country advertise nationally for summer help. Check the classifieds of vacation and travel magazines, and visit http://www.resortjobs.com for a listing. You could also select a resort and spa from the pages of a tourism publication, such as *Resorts and Great Hotels* (http://www.resortsgreathotels.com), and call the hotel directly to request information about summer jobs. *Spa Finder* (http://www.spafinders.com) magazine also publishes a directory of spas.

If you are unable to find a job at a spa, consider a part-time or summer job at a local hotel, beauty salon, or tanning salon. In any of these locations you will gain experience working with guests and providing for their comfort. Nursing homes and hospitals also employ high school students to provide clients or patients with personal care services. Working at a retail store specializing in products for skin care and beauty, aromatherapy, and massage can teach you about various spa treatments and products and help you decide if you are interested in this line of work.

If you have the money, consider making an appointment for yourself at a spa in your area. You may not be able to afford a vacation or full-day treatment, but even an hour spent as a client at a spa can give you an impression of what working in such an environment would be like.

EMPLOYERS

The International SPA Association estimates that, as of 2004, 280,700 people worked in the spa industry in the United States, which is up from 151,000 in 1999. Spas have grown at a very rapid rate over the past decade, and they should continue to do so as more people begin to value the benefits of spa visits. The primary employers of spa attendants are hotels, resorts, salons, and, naturally, spas.

Increasing numbers of salons are adding spas to their facilities to maintain a competitive edge; this will lead to increased opportunities for spa attendants throughout the country, mostly in larger cities and metropolitan areas. The same is true for hotel spas. Many spas, however, are clustered in resort areas with attractions like hot springs and consistently pleasant climates.

STARTING OUT

Many spa attendants receive their training on the job, but some background experience in health care or cosmetology may help you in landing that first job as a spa attendant. Craig Rabago, for example, worked as a surgical aide before going to work for the Ihilani. "The work is related," he says, "but it's a very different atmosphere." He learned about the spa job from a listing in the newspaper. If you're not particular about your geographic location, check travel publications for listings of resorts and spas, or visit http://www. spafinders.com on the Web, and contact the spas about job openings. *Spa Finder,* both online and in their print directory, lists spas according to their specialties and locations.

A degree from a cosmetology or massage therapy school can be valuable when looking for a job in a spa. Many of these degree programs require field work, or hands-on experience, and will put you in touch with salons and fitness centers. Without a degree, you may be limited in the spa treatments you're allowed to perform. But as more and more individual hair stylists and beauty salons open day spas to accommodate all the needs of their clients, both licensed and unlicensed spa attendants will find more job opportunities.

ADVANCEMENT

The longer an attendant works in a spa, the more he or she will learn about the services provided there. The attendant will also have more opportunities to expand upon the on-the-job training and potentially be allowed to perform more treatments. Though attendants typically start off with only an hourly wage, they can eventually receive commissions and tips. The more guests an attendant works with, the better tips and commission he or she will make. In a salon or day spa situation, the clientele will include regular customers. If they are happy with an attendant's work, they will request that attendant's services specifically and thus increase the attendant's income.

Attendants who complete further formal education also become qualified for more advanced positions. Those who attend cosmetology school to become cosmeticians typically take classes such as anatomy, chemistry, and physiology. They are qualified to work on the skin, giving facials, body wraps, and makeup applications, and may also do hair removal by waxing or plucking. Nail technician programs offered through cosmetology schools or nail schools qualify the graduate to give manicures and pedicures. Attendants who are particularly interested in fitness may want to consider advancement by getting an associate's degree from a fitness program. Courses for such programs include muscle conditioning, nutrition, and injury prevention. Those interested in massage may seek advancement by completing a massage therapy school program, which will qualify them to give different types of massage. These programs include course work in anatomy and physiology as well as provide hands-on training.

Some attendants advance to become spa program directors. As program directors, they are responsible for adding new services, training spa attendants, determining what skin products to use, and controlling other details of the spa's daily practices. Those who wish to run their own business may eventually open their own spa.

EARNINGS

Salaries for spa attendants vary greatly across the country, so no significant salary survey has been conducted in recent years. Spa attendants make from minimum wage to around $10 per hour. Salaries vary according to work environment (a large resort will pay more than a small salon) and the spa attendant's responsibilities. Spa attendants are either paid by the hour or by commission (a percentage of the spa treatments performed). Spa attendants also receive tips of between 10 and 15 percent. Some spas automatically bill guests an additional percentage to cover the tip, so that the guest doesn't have to worry about having the money on hand to give to the attendant. With tips from a wealthy clientele and a commission on higher priced services, a spa attendant at a fine hotel will make much more than an attendant in a smaller day spa. Employees of spas are likely to receive better benefits than many of their counterparts in the cosmetology field. Spa attendants working at hotels may also receive a variety of perks, such as discounted spa treatments, guest rooms, meals in the hotel restaurants, and travel packages.

WORK ENVIRONMENT

Working among vacationers in a sunny, scenic part of the world can be very enjoyable. Most spa attendants work within well-decorated, temperature-controlled buildings, with soothing music piped through the speaker systems. Fresh fruit, tea, and other refreshments are often readily available. Spa attendants work directly with a public that has come to a resort to alleviate stress and other worries, making for very relaxed interactions. Some hotel spa attendants even live on the premises in special employee quarters, or in nearby housing, allowing them to live close to the beaches, mountains, or whatever natural beauty surrounds the resort.

Because spas usually open in the wee hours of the morning and close after dark, spa attendants may have to work long, irregular hours. Depending on the codes of the spa, they wear uniforms and jackets. They also wear gloves if their skin is sensitive to some of the products.

In a local beauty salon, a spa attendant tries to maintain a similarly relaxed environment in the few rooms dedicated to spa treatment. The rest of the salon, however, may be noisy, with waiting customers, hair dryers, electric clippers, and music. The salon may also affect those with allergies to chemicals in hair treatment products.

Day spas, which may be located in large cities, typically strive to maintain a serene environment for the clientele, from the reception area, where soft music may be playing in the background, to the private treatment rooms, which may have soft lighting. While the spa attendant may work in these areas, he or she is also part of the activity behind the scenes, often working with damp laundry, cleaning supplies, and spa products.

OUTLOOK

The International SPA Association reports that there were 136 million spa visits in the United States in 2003—a decrease of approximately 17 million visits since 2001. Despite this decline, industry employment has remained steady, and the industry had revenue of $11.2 billion in 2003. Major trends in the industry include the growing popularity of medical, resort/hotel, and day spas, and the increasing popularity of spas among men. In fact, many spas are adding treatments specifically for men. These expanding facilities and new treatment options should translate into job opportunities for everyone working in this industry, including spa attendants.

In addition, the public is becoming more health conscious, and people are looking to spas for both enjoyable and educational vacations. Some spas are specializing in teaching guests new patterns of diet, exercise, and skin care. A number of health care professionals are even predicting that spas will be covered by health insurance plans; doctors will write prescriptions to patients for spa treatments. To compete with other spas, and to satisfy returning guests, spas are likely to offer even more diverse lists of services and treatments. The spa attendant will have to keep ahead of health and beauty trends and be capable of adapting to new programs and methods.

Anticipating a future of one-stop beauty treatment, the owners of hair and beauty salons are dedicating rooms to spa treatments. For the cost of a little remodeling, hair salons can stay competitive with local day spas, as well as generate more business. Spa attendants may find their best job opportunities at these salons, where they can earn a good commission and establish a client base.

FOR MORE INFORMATION

For information on day spas, contact
Day Spa Association
310 17th Street
Union City, NJ 07087-4310
Tel: 201-865-2065
Email: info@dayspaassociation.com
http://www.dayspaassociation.com

For more information on the spa industry, contact
International SPA Association
2365 Harrodsburg Road, Suite A325
Lexington, KY 40504-3366
Tel: 888-651-4772
Email: ispa@ispastaff.com
http://www.experienceispa.com

For information on accredited cosmetology schools and financial aid, contact
National Accrediting Commission of Cosmetology Arts and Sciences
4401 Ford Avenue, Suite 1300
Alexandria, VA 22302-1432
Tel: 703-600-7600
http://www.naccas.org

Tailors and Dressmakers

OVERVIEW

Tailors and *dressmakers* cut, sew, mend, and alter clothing. Typically, tailors work only with menswear, such as suits, jackets, and coats, while dressmakers work with women's clothing, including dresses, blouses, suits, evening wear, wedding and bridesmaids' gowns, and sportswear. Tailors and dressmakers are employed in dressmaking and custom-tailor shops, department stores, and garment factories; others are self-employed. Tailors, dressmakers, and sewers hold about 85,000 jobs in the United States.

HISTORY

The practice of making and wearing clothing evolved from the need for warmth and protection from injury. For example, in prehistoric times, people wrapped themselves in the warm skins of animals they had killed for food. Throughout history, both men and women, in all cultures and every economic and social class, have created clothing.

Early clothing styles developed according to the climate of the geographical area: skirts and loose blouses of thin fabrics in warmer climates, pants and coats of heavier fabrics in cold climates. Religious customs and occupations also affected clothing styles. But as civilizations grew more and more advanced, clothing as necessity evolved into clothing as fashion.

The invention of the spinning wheel, in use in the 12th century, sped the process of making threads and yarns. With the invention of the two-bar loom, fabric making increased, styles became more detailed, and clothing became more widely available. Fabric production further increased with other inventions, such as the spinning jenny that could spin more than one thread at a time, power looms that ran on steam, and the cotton gin. The invention of the sewing machine tremendously sped the production of garments, although tailors and dressmakers were never completely replaced by machines.

During the industrial revolution, factories replaced craft shops. High-production apparel companies employed hundreds of workers. Employees worked 12- to 14-hour workdays for low hourly pay in crowded rooms with poor ventilation and lighting. The poor working conditions of these factories, known as "sweatshops," led to the founding of the International Ladies Garment Workers Union in 1900 and the Amalgamated Clothing Workers of America in 1914; these unions protected workers' rights, ensured their safety, and led to greatly improved working conditions.

Today, the precise skills of tailors and dressmakers are still in demand at factories, stores, and small shops. The limited investment required to cut and sew garments, the wide availability of fabrics, and the demand for one-of-a-kind, tailor-made garments are factors that continue to provide opportunities for self-employed tailors and dressmakers.

THE JOB

Some tailors and dressmakers make garments from start to completion. In larger shops, however, each employee usually works on a specific task, such as measuring, patternmaking, cutting, fitting, or stitching. One worker, for example, may only sew in sleeves or pad lapels. Smaller shops may only measure and fit the garment, then send piecework to outside contractors. Some tailors and dressmakers specialize in one type of garment, such as suits or wedding gowns. Many also do alterations on factory-made clothing.

Tailors and dressmakers may run their own business, work in small shops, or work in the custom-tailoring section of large department stores. Some work out of their home. Retail clothing stores, specialty stores, bridal shops, and dry cleaners also employ tailors and dressmakers to do alterations.

Tailors and dressmakers first help customers choose the garment style and fabric, using their knowledge of the various types of fabrics. They take the customer's measurements, such as height, shoulder width, arm length, and waist, and they note any special figure problems. They may use ready-made paper patterns or make one of their own. The patterns are then placed on the fabric, and the fabric pieces are carefully cut. When the garment design is complex, or if there are special fitting problems, the tailor or dressmaker may cut the pattern from inexpensive muslin and fit it to the customer; any adjustments are then marked and transferred to the paper pattern before it is used to cut the actual garment fabric. The pieces are basted together first and then sewn by hand or machine. After one or two fittings, which confirm that the garment fits the customer properly, the tailor or dressmaker finishes the garment with hems, buttons, trim, and a final pressing.

Some tailors or dressmakers specialize in a certain aspect of the garment-making process. *Bushelers* work in factories to repair flaws and correct imperfect sewing in finished garments. *Shop tailors* have a detailed knowledge of special tailoring tasks. They use shears or a knife to trim and shape the edges of garments before sewing, attach shoulder pads, and sew linings in coats. *Skilled tailors* put fine stitching on lapels and pockets, make buttonholes, and sew on trim.

REQUIREMENTS

High School

While in high school, you should get as much experience as you can by taking any sewing, tailoring, and clothing classes offered by vocational or home economics departments. There are also a number of institutions that offer either on-site or home-study courses in sewing and dressmaking. Art classes in sketching and design are also helpful. Math classes, such as algebra and geometry, will help you hone your ability to work with numbers and to visualize shapes.

Postsecondary Training

Tailors and dressmakers must have at least a high school education, although employers prefer college graduates with advanced training in sewing, tailoring, draping, patternmaking, and design. A limited number of schools and colleges in the United States offer this type of training, including Philadelphia University, the Fashion Institute of Technology in New York City, and the Parsons School of Design, also in New York. Students who are interested in furthering their career, and perhaps expanding from tailoring into design, may want to consider studying in one of these specialized institutions. It is, however, entirely possible to enter this field without a college degree.

Other Requirements

Workers in this field must obviously have the ability to sew very well, both by hand and machine, follow directions, and measure accurately. In addition to these skills, tailors and dressmakers must have a good eye for color and style. They need to know how to communicate with and satisfy customers. Strong interpersonal skills will help tailors and dressmakers get and keep clients.

EXPLORING

Take sewing classes at school. Also, check with your local park district or fabric and craft stores—they often offer lessons year-round. Find summer or part-time employment at a local tailor shop. This will give you valuable work experience. Contact schools regarding their programs in fashion design. If their course descriptions sound interesting, take a class or two. You can also create and sew your own designs or offer your mending and alteration services to your family and friends. Finally, visit department stores, clothing specialty stores, and tailor's shops to observe workers involved in this field.

EMPLOYERS

Approximately 85,000 tailors, dressmakers, and sewers are employed in the United States. Those interested in high fashion should check out haute couture houses such as Chanel or Yves Saint Laurent. These industry giants deal with expensive fabrics and innovative designs. They also cater to a high level of clientele. Be prepared for stiff competition because such businesses will consider only the most experienced, highly skilled tailors and dressmakers.

Tailors and dressmakers employed at retail department stores make alterations on ready-to-wear clothing sold on the premises. They may perform a small task such as hemming pants or suit sleeves or a major project such as custom fitting a wedding dress.

In some cases, it is possible for tailors or dressmakers to start their own businesses by making clothes and taking orders from those who like their work. Capital needed to start such a venture is minimal, since the most important equipment, such as a sewing machine, iron and ironing board, scissors, and notions, are widely available and relatively inexpensive. Unless the tailor or dressmaker plans to operate a home-based business, however, he or she will need to rent shop space. Careful planning is needed to prepare for a self-owned tailoring or dressmaking business. Anyone running a business needs to

Mean Annual Earnings by Industry, 2005

Employer	Mean Annual Earnings
Apparel and piece goods merchant wholesalers	$32,510
Department stores	$29,130
Clothing stores	$25,820
Cut and sew apparel manufacturing	$25,490
Dry cleaning and laundry services	$21,770
Household goods repair and maintenance	$20,760

Source: U.S. Department of Labor

learn bookkeeping, accounting, and how to keep and order supplies. Knowledge of marketing is important too, since the owner of a business must know how, when, and where to advertise in order to attract customers. Tailors or dressmakers planning to start their own business should check with their library or local government to learn what requirements, such as permits, apply. Finally, don't forget to consult established tailors and dressmakers to learn the tricks of the trade.

STARTING OUT

Custom-tailor shops or garment-manufacturing centers sometimes offer apprenticeships to students or recent graduates, which give them a start in the business. As a beginner, you may also find work in related jobs, such as a sewer or alterer in a custom-tailoring or dressmaking shop, garment factory, dry-cleaning store, or department store. Apply directly to such companies and shops and monitor local newspaper ads for openings as well. Check with your high school's career center to see if it has any industry information or leads for part-time jobs. Trade schools and colleges that have programs in textiles or fashion often offer their students help with job placement.

ADVANCEMENT

Workers in this field usually start by performing simple tasks. As they gain more experience and their skills improve, they may be assigned to more difficult and complicated tasks. Advancement in the industry is typically somewhat limited, though. In factories, a production worker might be promoted to the position of line supervisor. Tailors and dressmakers can move to a better shop that offers higher pay or open their own business.

Some workers may find that they have an eye for color and style and an aptitude for design. With further training at an appropriate college, these workers may find a successful career in fashion design and merchandising.

EARNINGS

Salaries for tailors and dressmakers vary widely, depending on experience, skill, and location. The median annual salary for tailors, dressmakers, and custom sewers reported by the U.S. Department of Labor in 2005 was $10.95, or $22,770 a year for full-time work. The lowest paid 10 percent earned less than $15,270 a year, while the highest paid 10 percent earned more than $35,850 annually.

Workers employed by large companies and retail stores receive benefits such as paid holidays and vacations, health insurance, and pension plans. They are often affiliated with the labor union UNITE HERE, which may offer additional benefits. Self-employed tailors and dressmakers and small-shop workers usually provide their own benefits.

WORK ENVIRONMENT

Tailors and dressmakers in large shops work 40 to 48 hours a week, sometimes including Saturdays. Union members usually work 35 to 40 hours a week. Those who run their own businesses often work longer hours. Spring and fall are usually the busiest times.

Since tailoring and dressmaking require a minimal investment, some tailors and dressmakers work out of their homes. Those who work in the larger apparel plants may find the conditions less pleasant. The noise of the machinery can be nerve-wracking, the dye from the fabric may be irritating to the eyes and the skin, and some factories are old and not well maintained.

Much of the work is done sitting down, in one location, and may include fine detail work that can be time consuming. The work may be tiring and tedious and occasionally can cause eyestrain. In some cases, tailors and dressmakers deal directly with customers, who may be either pleasant to interact with or difficult and demanding.

This type of work, however, can be very satisfying to people who enjoy using their hands and skills to create something. It can be gratifying to complete a project properly, and many workers in this field take great pride in their workmanship.

OUTLOOK

According to the U.S. Department of Labor, employment prospects in this industry are expected to decline through 2014. Factors attributing to the decline include the low cost and ready availability of factory-made clothing and the invention of laborsaving machinery such as computerized sewing and cutting machines. In fact, automated machines are expected to replace many sewing jobs in the next decade. In addition, the apparel industry has declined domestically as many businesses choose to produce their items abroad, where labor is cheap and often unregulated.

Tailors and dressmakers who do reliable and skillful work, however, particularly in the areas of mending and alterations, should be able to find employment. This industry is large, employing thousands of people. Many job openings will be created as current employees leave the workforce due to retirement or other reasons.

FOR MORE INFORMATION

For information on careers in the apparel-manufacturing industry, contact
American Apparel and Footwear Association
1601 North Kent Street, Suite 1200
Arlington, VA 22209-2105
Tel: 800-520-2262
http://www.apparelandfootwear.org

For information on custom tailoring, contact
Custom Tailors and Designers Association of America
19 Mantua Road
Mt. Royal, NJ 08061-1006
Tel: 856-423-1621
http://www.ctda.com

For a listing of home-study institutions offering sewing and dress-making courses, contact
Distance Education and Training Council
1601 18th Street, NW, Suite 2
Washington, DC 20009-2529

Tel: 202-234-5100
Email: detc@detc.org
http://www.detc.org

For information packets on college classes in garment design and sewing, contact the following schools:

Fashion Institute of Design and Merchandising
919 South Grand Avenue
Los Angeles, CA 90015-1421
Tel: 800-624-1200
http://www.fidm.com

Fashion Institute of Technology
Seventh Avenue at 27th Street
New York, NY 10001-5992
Tel: 212-217-7999
Email: FITinfo@fitnyc.edu
http://www.fitnyc.edu

Parsons School of Design
66 Fifth Avenue
New York, NY 10011-8802
Tel: 800-252-0852
http://www.parsons.edu

Philadelphia University
School House Lane and Henry Avenue
Philadelphia, PA 19144-5497
Tel: 215-951-2700
http://www.philau.edu

For career information, visit the following Web site:

Career Threads
http://careerthreads.com

Taxidermists

OVERVIEW

Taxidermists preserve and prepare animal skins and parts to create lifelike animal replicas. Taxidermists prepare the underpadding and mounting that the skin will be attached to, model the structure to resemble the animal's body, and then attach appropriate coverings, such as skin, fur, or feathers. They may add details, such as eyes or teeth, to make a more realistic representation. The animals they mount or stuff may be for private or public display. Museums frequently use creations from taxidermists to display rare, exotic, or extinct animals. Hunters also use taxidermists' services to mount fishing and hunting trophies for display.

HISTORY

Animal tanning and skin preservation has been practiced over the millennia for clothing, decoration, and weapons. Native Americans used tanned hides to make their lodgings. Trophies from hunts of dangerous animals were often worn to display the bravery of the hunter. Tanning methods included stringing skins up to dry, scraping them, and perhaps soaking them in water with tannins from leaves. Animal skins were preserved for many different purposes, but not specifically from interest in the natural sciences until the 18th century. Tanning methods improved during this time. Displaying the skin on models stuffed with hay or straw became popular for museums and private collections. Animals were posed realistically, and backgrounds were added to the display areas in museums to show the habitat of the animal.

By the 19th century, taxidermy was a recognized discipline for museum workers. In Paris, Maison Verreaux became the chief supplier of exhibit animals. Carl Akeley, who worked for Ward's Natural Science Establishment in New York, mastered a taxidermic technique that allowed for realistic modeling of large animals such as bears, lions, and elephants. His works are still on display in the Chicago Field Museum of Natural History and the New York Natural History Museum. In recent years, several taxidermy supply companies have developed lifelike mannequins to be used as the foundation for fish, birds, and fur-bearing animals. Such new techniques in the art and science of taxidermy continue to be developed and used.

THE JOB

Taxidermists use a variety of methods to create realistic, lifelike models of birds and animals. Although specific processes and techniques vary, most taxidermists follow a series of basic steps.

First, they must remove the skin from the carcass of the animal with special knives, scissors, and pliers. The skin must be removed very carefully to preserve the natural state of the fur or feathers. Once the skin is removed, it is preserved with a special solution.

Some taxidermists still make the body foundation, or skeleton, of the animal. These foundations are made with a variety of materials, including clay, plaster, burlap, papier-mâché, wire mesh, and glue. Other taxidermists, however, use ready-made forms, which are available in various sizes; taxidermists simply take measurements of the specimen to be mounted and order the proper size from the supplier. Metal rods are often used to achieve the desired mount of the animal.

The taxidermist uses special adhesives or modeling clay to attach the skin to the foundation or form. Then artificial eyes, teeth, and tongues are attached. Sometimes taxidermists use special techniques, such as airbrushing color or sculpting the eyelids, nose, and lips. They may need to attach antlers, horns, or claws. Finally, they groom and dress the fur or feathers with styling gel, if necessary, to enhance the final appearance of the specimen.

Taxidermists work with a variety of animal types, including one-cell organisms, large game animals, birds, fish, and reptiles. They even make models of extinct animal species, based on detailed drawings or paintings. The specific work often depends on the area of the country where the taxidermist is employed, since the types of animals hunted vary by region.

REQUIREMENTS

High School

High school classes in art, woodworking, and metal shop may help develop the skills necessary for this career. Also, a class or classes in biology might be helpful for learning the bodily workings of certain animals.

Postsecondary Training

In the United States, several schools offer programs or correspondence courses in taxidermy. Courses often last from four to six weeks, and subjects such as laws and legalities, bird mounting, fish mounting, deer, small mammals, diorama-making, airbrush painting, and form-making are covered. Taxidermists who hope to work in museums should expect to take further training and acquire additional skills in related subjects, which they can learn in museum classes.

Self-employed taxidermists need accounting, advertising, and marketing courses to help in the management of a business, including maintaining an inventory of chemicals and supplies, advertising and promotion, and pricing their work.

Certification or Licensing

Taxidermists are required to be licensed in most states, with specific licensing requirements varying from state to state. Many taxidermists choose to become members of national or local professional associations. The largest of these, the National Taxidermists Association, offers the designation of certified taxidermist to members who have met specific requirements. Members may be certified in one or all four categories of specialization: mammals, fish, birds, and reptiles. Certification indicates that they have reached a certain level of expertise and may allow them to charge a higher price for their work.

Other Requirements

Successful taxidermy requires many skills. You must have good manual dexterity, an eye for detail, knowledge of animal anatomy, and training in the taxidermy processes.

EXPLORING

Because taxidermy is a specialized occupation, there are few opportunities for part-time or summer work for students,

Learn More About It

Browne, Montagu. *Practical Taxidermy: A Manual of Instruction to the Amateur in Collecting, Preserving, and Setting up Natural History Specimens of All Kinds.* Cookhill, U.K.: Read Country Books, 2005.

Burch, Monte. *The Ultimate Guide to Skinning and Tanning: A Complete Guide to Working with Pelts, Fur, and Leather.* Guilford, Conn.: The Lyons Press, 2002.

Grantz, Gerald. *Home Book of Taxidermy and Tanning.* Mechanicsburg, Pa.: Stackpole Books, 1985.

Tinsley, Russell. *Taxidermy Guide* 3rd ed. Accokeek, Md.: Stoeger Publishing Company, 1990.

Triplett, Todd. *Big-Game Taxidermy: A Complete Guide to Deer, Antelope, and Elk.* Guilford, Conn.: The Lyons Press, 2006.

Triplett, Todd. *The Complete Guide to Small Game Taxidermy: How to Work with Squirrels, Varmints, and Predators.* Guilford, Conn.: The Lyons Press, 2003.

although some larger companies hire apprentices to help with the workload. You may learn more, however, by ordering videotapes and beginners' mounting kits to experience the mounting process. Other good learning opportunities include speaking to a museum taxidermist or writing to schools or associations that offer courses in taxidermy. Check with the National Taxidermists Association for upcoming conventions and seminars that are open to the public. Time spent at such an event would provide not only a solid learning experience, but also a chance to meet and mingle with the pros.

EMPLOYERS

Taxidermists can be found throughout the United States and abroad. Experienced and established taxidermists, especially those with a large client base, will often hire apprentices, or less experienced taxidermists, to assist with larger projects or to undertake smaller jobs. Contact the National Taxidermists Association for a listing of such employers. The majority of taxidermists, about 70 to 80 percent, are self-employed.

STARTING OUT

Taxidermy is a profession that requires experience. Most workers start out as hobbyists in their own homes, and eventually start doing taxidermy work professionally on a part-time basis. Later, after they have built up a client base, they may enter the profession full time. Jobs in existing taxidermy shops or businesses are difficult to find because most taxidermists are self-employed and prefer to do the work themselves. In some cases, however, it may be possible to become a journeyman or apprentice and work for an already established taxidermist on either an hourly basis or for a percentage of the selling price of the work they are doing.

Jobs in museums are often difficult to obtain; applicants should have a background in both taxidermy and general museum studies. Taxidermy schools primarily train their students to become self-employed but may sometimes offer job placement as well.

ADVANCEMENT

Advancement opportunities are good for those with the proper skills, education, and experience. Taxidermists who can work on a wide range of projects will have the best chances of advancing. Since larger game animals bring more money, one method of advancing would be to learn the skills necessary to work on these animals. Taxidermists who develop a large customer base may open their own shop. Workers employed in museums may advance to positions with more responsibilities and higher pay.

EARNINGS

A taxidermist's level of experience, certification, speed, and quality of work are all factors that significantly affect income. Most taxidermists will charge by the inch or the weight of the animal. Fees can range from $100 to $2,500, depending on the size of the animal and the style of the mount. Difficult mounts or unusual background accessories may add significantly to the final price. For example, an open mouth on an animal, as opposed to a droopy mouth or a closed mouth, can add about $100 to the price of a mounting. In addition, the region of the country and the type of game typically hunted and mounted are important variables. Most new taxidermists might expect to earn about $15,000 annually. Those with five to 10 years of experience and proven skills can earn $30,000 or more. Some exceptional taxidermists can earn upwards of $50,000 annually. Museum workers might also expect to average $25,000 to $30,000 yearly.

Because most taxidermists are self-employed or work for a very small operation, few have any sort of benefits package. Those who work in museums, however, may be offered health insurance and paid vacation and sick leave.

WORK ENVIRONMENT

Most taxidermists work 40 hours a week, although overtime is not uncommon during certain times of the year. Taxidermists with their own shops may have to work long hours, especially when first starting out. They often work with strong chemicals, glues, hand and power tools, and possibly diseased animals. If working on smaller animals and birds, they can sit or stand. Creating larger mammal displays, however, requires more physical work, such as climbing or squatting.

Workers in taxidermy will find it satisfying to see a project from beginning to completion. There is also the element of pride in good craftsmanship; it can be gratifying for workers to use their talents to recreate extremely realistic and lifelike animal forms.

OUTLOOK

The job outlook for taxidermists should be good over the next decade. Although jobs in museums may be scarce, the demand for hunting and fishing trophies continues to provide work for taxidermists. It is not unusual for qualified taxidermists to have a year's worth of work backlogged. In addition, many educational institutions actively seek models of animal and bird species that are nearing extinction. Talented taxidermists who can take on a variety of projects should be able to find steady employment. Those with an eye for unique poses and mounts, or unusual expressions, will be in high demand.

FOR MORE INFORMATION

For information on the industry, certification, taxidermy schools, trade magazines, association membership, and career opportunities, contact

National Taxidermists Association
108 Branch Drive
Slidell, LA 70461-1912

Tel: 866-662-9054
Email: ntahq@aol.com
http://www.nationaltaxidermists.com

For information on training in taxidermy, including a list of schools, workshops, books, magazines, videos, and links to state taxidermy associations, visit
Taxidermy.net
http://www.taxidermy.net

Taxi Drivers

OVERVIEW

Taxi drivers, also known as *cab drivers,* operate automobiles and other motor vehicles to take passengers from one place to another for a fee. This fee is usually based on distance traveled or time, as recorded on a taximeter. There are currently about 188,000 taxi drivers and chauffeurs in the United States.

HISTORY

Today's taxis are the modern equivalent of vehicles for hire that were first introduced in England in the early 1600s. These vehicles were hackneys, which were four-wheeled carriages drawn by two horses that could carry up to six passengers. By 1654, there were already 300 privately owned hackneys licensed to operate in London. In the next century, hackneys were introduced in the United States. Around 1820, a smaller vehicle for hire, the cabriolet, became common in London. At first it had two wheels, with room only for a driver and one passenger, and one horse drew it. Some later cabriolets, or cabs, as they were soon called, were larger, and by mid-century, a two-passenger version, the hansom cab, became the most popular cab in London. Hansom cabs were successfully brought to New York and Boston in the 1870s.

Toward the end of the 19th century, motorized cabs began to appear in the streets of Europe and America. From then on, the development of cabs paralleled the development of the automobile. The earliest motorized cabs were powered by electricity, but cabs with internal combustion engines appeared by the early 20th century. Along with the introduction of these vehicles came the need for drivers, thus creating the cab driver profession. In 1891, a device called a "taximeter" (tax is from a Latin word meaning "charge") was invented to calculate the fare owed to the driver. Taximeters found their first use in the new horseless carriages for hire, which were soon called "taxicabs" or just "taxis."

The use of taxis has increased especially in metropolitan areas, where there is dense traffic, increasing population, and limited parking. Modern taxis are often four-door passenger cars that have been specially modified. Depending on local regulations, the vehicles may have such modifications as reinforced frames or extra heavy-duty shock absorbers. Taxi drivers may be employees of taxi companies, driving cars owned by the company; they may be lease drivers, operating cars leased from a taxi company for a regular fee; or they may be completely independent, driving cars that they own themselves.

THE JOB

Taxicabs are an important part of the mass transportation system in many cities, so drivers need to be familiar with as much of the local geographical area as possible. But taxicab drivers are often required to do more than simply drive people from one place to another. They also help people with their luggage. Sometimes they pick up and deliver packages. Some provide sightseeing tours for visitors to a community.

Taxi drivers who are employed by, or lease from, a cab service or garage report to the garage before their shift begins and are assigned a cab. They receive a trip sheet and record their name, date of work, and identification number. They also perform a quick, cursory check of the interior and exterior of the car to ensure its proper working condition. They check fuel and oil levels, brakes, lights, and windshield wipers, reporting any problems to the dispatcher or company mechanic.

Taxi drivers locate passengers in three ways. Customers requiring transportation may call the cab company with the approximate time and place at they wish to be picked up. The dispatcher uses a two-way radio system to notify the driver of this pick-up information. Other drivers pick up passengers at cabstands and taxi lines at airports, theaters, hotels, and railroad stations, and then return to the stand after they deliver the passengers. Drivers may pick up passengers while returning to their stands or stations. The third manner of pick up for taxi drivers is by cruising busy streets to service passengers who hail or "wave them down."

When a destination is reached, the taxi driver determines the fare and informs the rider of the cost. Fares consist of many parts. The drop charge is an automatic charge for use of the cab. Other parts of the fare are determined by the time and distance traveled. The taximeter measures the fare as it accrues. The driver turns this machine on when the passenger enters the cab, and off when he or she exits. Additional portions of the fare may include charges for luggage handling and additional occupants. Commonly, a passenger will offer the taxi driver a tip, which is based on the customer's opinion of the quality and efficiency of the ride and the courtesy of the driver. The taxi driver also may supply a receipt if the passenger requests it.

Taxi drivers are required to keep accurate records of their activities. They record the time and place where they picked up and delivered the passengers on a trip sheet. They also have to keep records on the amount of fares they collect.

There are taxis and taxi drivers in almost every town and city in the country, but most are in large metropolitan areas.

REQUIREMENTS

High School

Taxi drivers do not usually need to meet any particular educational requirements, but a high school education will help you adequately handle the record-keeping part of the job. You should also take courses in driver education, business math, and English.

Certification or Licensing

In large cities, some taxi drivers belong to labor unions. The union to which most belong is the International Brotherhood of Teamsters.

Those interested in becoming a taxi driver must have a regular driver's license. In most large cities, taxi drivers also must have a special taxicab operator's license—commonly called a hack's license—in addition to a chauffeur's license. Police departments, safety departments, or public utilities commissions generally issue these special licenses. To secure the license, drivers must pass special examinations that include questions on local geography, traffic regulations, accident reports, safe driving practices, and insurance regulations. Some companies help their job applicants prepare for these examinations by providing them with specially prepared booklets. The operator's license may need to be renewed annually. In some cities (New York, for example), new license applications can take several months to be processed because the applicant's background must be investigated. Increasingly, many cities and municipalities require a test on English usage. Those who do not pass must take a course in English sponsored by the municipality.

Other Requirements

If you plan on becoming a taxi driver, you should be in reasonably good health and have a good driving record and no criminal record. In general, you must be 21 years of age or older to drive a taxicab. While driving is not physically strenuous, you will occasionally be asked to lift heavy packages or luggage. If you work in a big city, you should have especially steady nerves because you will spend considerable time driving in heavy traffic. You must also be courteous, patient, and able to get along with many different kinds of people.

Taxi drivers who own their own cab or lease one for a long period of time are generally expected to keep their cab clean. Large companies have workers who take care of this task for all the vehicles in the company fleet.

EXPLORING

Visit your local library to find books about taxi drivers and other transportation careers. Ask your teacher or guidance counselor to set up a talk with a taxi driver. Take a ride in a taxi to experience the career firsthand.

EMPLOYERS

Approximately 188,000 taxi drivers and chauffeurs are employed in the United States. Taxi drivers are often employed by a cab service and drive cars owned by the company. Some drivers pay a fee and lease cabs owned by a taxi company, while others (about 27 percent) own and operate their own cars.

STARTING OUT

Usually people who want to be taxi drivers apply directly to taxicab companies that may be hiring new drivers. Taxicab companies are usually listed in the Yellow Pages. It may take some time to obtain the necessary license to drive a cab, and some companies or municipalities may require additional training, so it may not be possible to begin work immediately. People who have sufficient funds may buy their own cab, but they usually must secure a municipal permit to operate it.

EARNINGS

Earnings for taxi drivers vary widely, depending on the number of hours they work, the method by which they are paid, the season, the weather, and other factors. Median hourly earnings of salaried taxi drivers and chauffeurs, including tips, were $9.60 in 2005, according to the U.S. Department of Labor. Wages ranged from less than $6.68 to more than $15.23 an hour.

Limited information suggests that independent owner-drivers can average anywhere from $20,000 to $30,000 annually, including tips. This assumes they work the industry average of eight to 10 hours a day, five days a week. Many chauffeurs who work full time earn from about $25,000 to $50,000, including tips.

Many taxi drivers are paid a percentage of the fares they collect, often 40 to 50 percent of total fares. Other drivers receive a base amount plus a commission related to the amount of business they do. A few drivers are guaranteed minimum daily or weekly wages. Drivers who lease their cabs may keep all the fare money above the amount of the leasing fee they pay the cab company. Tips are also an important part of the earnings of taxi drivers; they can equal 15 to 20 percent or more of total fares. Most taxi drivers do not receive company-provided fringe benefits, such as pension plans.

Earnings fluctuate with the season and the weather. Winter is generally the busiest season, and snow and rain almost always produce a busy day. There is also a relationship between general economic conditions and the earnings of taxi drivers, because there is more competition for less business when the economy is in a slump.

WORK ENVIRONMENT

Many taxi drivers put in long hours, working from eight to 12 hours a day, five or six days a week. They do not receive overtime pay. Other drivers are part-time workers. Drivers may work Sundays, holidays, or evening hours.

Taxi drivers must be able to get along with their passengers, including those who try their patience or expect too much. Some people urge drivers to go very fast, for example, but drivers who comply may risk accidents or arrests for speeding. Drivers may have to work under other difficult conditions, such as heavy traffic and bad weather. Taxi drivers must be able to drive safely under pressure. In some places, drivers must be wary because there is a considerable chance of being robbed.

OUTLOOK

There will always be a need for taxi drivers. Job opportunities for taxi drivers are expected to grow faster than the average for all occupations through 2014, according to the U.S. Department of Labor. The high turnover rate in this occupation means that many of the new job openings that develop in the future will come when drivers leave their jobs to go into another kind of work. In addition, as the American population increases and traffic becomes more congested, the need for taxi drivers will increase, especially in metropolitan areas. At present, many drivers work on a part-time basis, and that situation is likely to continue.

FOR MORE INFORMATION

For additional information about the taxi driving profession, contact
Taxicab, Limousine and Paratransit Association
3849 Farragut Avenue
Kensington, MD 20895-2004
Tel: 301-946-5701
Email: info@tlpa.org
http://www.tlpa.org

Tax Preparers

OVERVIEW

Tax preparers prepare income tax returns for individuals and small businesses for a fee, for either quarterly or yearly filings. They help to establish and maintain business records to expedite tax preparations and may advise clients on how to save money on their tax payments. There are approximately 86,000 tax preparers employed in the United States.

HISTORY

President Franklin D. Roosevelt once said, "Taxes are the dues that we pay for the privileges of membership in an organized society." Although most people grumble about paying income taxes and filling out tax forms, everyone carries a share of the burden, and it is still possible to keep a sense of humor about income taxes. As Benjamin Franklin succinctly said, "In this world nothing can be said to be certain, except death and taxes."

While the personal income tax may be the most familiar type of taxation, it is actually a relatively recent method of raising revenue. To raise funds for the Napoleonic Wars between 1799 and 1816, Britain became the first nation to collect income taxes, but a permanent income tax was not established there until 1874. In the same manner, the United States first initiated a temporary income tax during the Civil War. It wasn't until 1913, however, with the adoption of the 16th Amendment to the Constitution, that a tax on personal income became the law of the nation. In addition to the federal income tax, many states and cities have adopted income tax laws. Income taxes are an example of a "progressive

QUICK FACTS

School Subjects
Business
Mathematics

Personal Skills
Following instructions
Helping/teaching

Work Environment
Primarily indoors
Primarily one location

Minimum Education Level
Some postsecondary training

Salary Range
$15,780 to $25,700 to
$52,860+

Certification or Licensing
Required by certain states

Outlook
About as fast as the average

DOT
219

GOE
07.02.02

NOC
1431

O*NET-SOC
13-2082.00

tax," one that charges higher percentages of income as people earn more money.

Technology has now made it possible to file taxes electronically. Electronic tax filing is a method by which a tax return is converted to computer-readable form and sent via modem to the Internal Revenue Service. Electronically filed tax returns are more accurate than paper-filed returns because of the extensive checking performed by the electronic-filing software. Detecting and correcting errors early also allows the tax return to flow smoothly through the IRS, speeding up the refund process. New computer software is also available that gives individuals a framework in which to prepare and file their own taxes.

THE JOB

Tax preparers help individuals and small businesses keep the proper records to determine their legally required tax and file the proper forms. They must be well acquainted with federal, state, and local tax laws and use their knowledge and skills to help taxpayers take the maximum number of legally allowable deductions.

The first step in preparing tax forms is to collect all the data and documents that are needed to calculate the client's tax liability. The client has to submit documents such as tax returns from previous years, wage and income statements, records of other sources of income, statements of interest and dividends earned, records of expenses, property tax records, and so on. The tax preparer then interviews the client to obtain further information that may have a bearing on the amount of tax owed. If the client is an individual taxpayer, the tax preparer will ask about any important investments, extra expenses that may be deductible, contributions to charity, and insurance payments; events such as marriage, childbirth, and new employment are also important considerations. If the client is a business, the tax preparer may ask about capital gains and losses, taxes already paid, payroll expenses, miscellaneous business expenses, and tax credits.

Once the tax preparer has a complete picture of the client's income and expenses, the proper tax forms and schedules needed in order to file the tax return can be determined. While some taxpayers have very complex finances that take a long time to document and calculate, others have typical, straightforward returns that take less time. Often, the tax preparer can calculate the amount a taxpayer owes, fill out the proper forms, and prepare the complete return in a single interview. When the tax return is more complicated, the tax preparer may have to collect all the data during the interview and perform the calculations later. If a client's taxes are unusual or very complex, the tax preparer may have to consult tax law handbooks and bulletins.

Computers are the main tools used to figure and prepare tax returns. The tax preparer inputs the data onto a spreadsheet, and the computer calculates and prints out the tax form. Computer software can be very versatile and may even print up data summary sheets that can serve as checklists and references for the next tax filing.

Tax preparers often have another tax expert or preparer check their work, especially if they work for a tax service firm. The second tax preparer will check to make sure the allowances and deductions taken were proper and that no others were overlooked. They also make certain that the tax laws are interpreted properly and that calculations are correct. It is very important that a tax preparer's work is accurate and error-free, and clients are given a guarantee covering additional taxes or fines if the preparer's work is found to be incorrect. Tax preparers are required by law to sign every return they complete for a client and provide their Social Security number or federal identification number. They must also provide the client with a copy of the tax return and keep a copy in their own files.

REQUIREMENTS

High School

Although there are no specific postsecondary educational require-ments for tax preparers, you should certainly get your high school diploma. While you are in high school, there are a number of classes you can take that will help prepare you for this type of work. Natu-rally, take mathematics classes. Accounting, bookkeeping, and busi-ness classes will also give you a feel for working with numbers and show you the importance of accurate work. In addition, take com-puter classes. You will need to be comfortable using computers, since much tax work is done using this tool. Finally, take English classes. English classes will help you work on your research, writing, and speaking skills—important communication skills to have when you work with clients.

Postsecondary Training

Once you have completed high school, you may be able to find a job as a tax preparer at a large tax-preparing firm. These firms, such as H&R Block, typically require their tax preparers to complete a training program in tax preparation. If you would like to pursue a college education, many universities offer individual courses and complete majors in the area of taxation. Another route is to earn a bachelor's degree or master's degree in business administration with a minor or concentration in taxation. A few universities offer master's degrees in taxation.

In addition to formal education, tax preparers must continue their professional education. Both federal and state tax laws are revised every year, and the tax preparer is obligated to understand these new laws thoroughly by January 1 of each year. Major tax reform legislation can increase this amount of study even further. One federal reform tax bill can take up thousands of pages, and this can mean up to 60 hours of extra study in a single month to fully understand all the intricacies and implications of the new laws. To help tax preparers keep up with new developments, the National Association of Tax Practitioners offers more than 200 workshops every year. Tax service firms also offer classes explaining tax preparation to both professionals and individual taxpayers.

Certification or Licensing

Licensing requirements for tax preparers vary by state, and you should be sure to find out what requirements there are in the state where you wish to practice. Since 2002, for example, tax preparers in California have been required to register with the California Tax Education Council, a nonprofit corporation established by the California State Legislature to oversee tax preparation. Tax preparers who apply for registration in that state must be at least 18 years old. In addition, they need to have 60 hours of formal, approved instruction in basic income tax law, theory, and practice, or two years of professional experience in preparing personal income tax returns.

The Internal Revenue Service (IRS) offers an examination for tax preparers. Those who complete the test successfully are called *enrolled agents* and are entitled to legally represent any taxpayer in any type of audit before the IRS or state tax boards. (Those with five years' experience working for the IRS as an auditor or in a higher position can become enrolled agents without taking the exam.) The four-part test is offered annually and takes two days to complete. There are no education or experience requirements for taking the examination, but the questions are roughly equivalent to those asked in a college course. Study materials and applications may be obtained from local IRS offices. The IRS does not oversee seasonal tax preparers, but local IRS offices may monitor some commercial tax offices.

The Institute of Tax Consultants offers an annual open-book exam to obtain the title of certified tax preparer (CTP). Certification also requires 30 hours of continuing education each year.

Other Requirements

Tax preparers should have an aptitude for math and an eye for detail. They should have strong organizational skills and the patience to sift through documents and financial statements. The ability to communicate effectively with clients is also key to being able to explain complex tax procedures and to making customers feel confident and comfortable. Tax preparers also need to work well under the stress and pressure of deadlines. They must also be honest, discreet, and trustworthy in dealing with the financial and business affairs of their clients.

EXPLORING

If a career in tax preparation sounds interesting, you should first gain some experience by completing income tax returns for yourself and for your family and friends. These returns should be double-checked by the actual taxpayers who will be liable for any fees and extra taxes if the return is prepared incorrectly. You can also look for internships or part-time jobs in tax service offices and tax preparation firms. Many of these firms operate nationwide, and extra office help might be needed as tax deadlines approach and work becomes hectic. The IRS also trains people to answer tax questions for its 800-number telephone advisory service; they are employed annually during early spring.

Try also to familiarize yourself with the tax preparation software available on the Internet and utilize Web sites to keep abreast of changing laws, regulations, and developments in the industry. The National Association of Tax Professionals offers sample articles from its publications, *TAXPRO Quarterly Journal* and *TAXPRO Monthly,* online. (See end of article for contact information.)

EMPLOYERS

Approximately 86,000 tax preparers are employed in the United States. Tax preparers may work for tax service firms such as H&R

Block and other similar companies that conduct most of their business during tax season. Other tax preparers may be self-employed and work full or part time.

STARTING OUT

Because tax work is very seasonal, most tax firms begin hiring tax preparers in December for the upcoming tax season. Some tax service firms will hire tax preparers from among the graduates of their own training courses. Private and state employment agencies may also have information and job listings, as will classified newspaper ads. You should also consult your school guidance offices to establish contacts in the field.

There are a large number of Internet sites for this industry, many of which offer job postings. Many large tax preparation firms, such as H & R Block, also have their own Web pages.

ADVANCEMENT

Some tax preparers may wish to continue their academic education and work toward becoming certified public accountants. Others may want to specialize in certain areas of taxation, such as real estate, corporate, or nonprofit work. Tax preparers who specialize in certain fields are able to charge higher fees for their services.

Establishing a private consulting business is also an option. Potential proprietors should consult with other self-employed practitioners to gain advice on how to start a private practice. Several Internet sites also give valuable advice on establishing a tax business.

EARNINGS

According to the U.S. Department of Labor, the median annual income for tax preparers was approximately $25,700 in 2005. Salaries ranged from less than $15,780 to more than $52,860 or more annually. Incomes can vary widely from these figures, however, due to a number of factors. One reason is that tax preparers generally charge a fee per tax return, which may range from $30 to $1,500 or more, depending on the complexity of the return and the preparation time required. Therefore, the number of clients a preparer has, as well as the difficulty of the returns, can affect the preparer's income. Another factor affecting income is the amount of education a tax preparer has. Seasonal or part-time employees, typically those with less education, usually earn minimum wage plus commission. Enrolled agents, certified public accountants, and other professional preparers, typically those with college degrees or more, usually charge more. Finally, it is important to realize that fees vary widely in different parts of the country. Tax preparers in large cities and in the eastern United States generally charge more, as do those who offer year-round financial advice and services.

WORK ENVIRONMENT

Tax preparers generally work in office settings that may be located in neighborhood business districts, shopping malls, or other high-traffic areas. Employees of tax service firms may work at storefront desks or in cubicles during the three months preceding the April 15 tax-filing deadline. In addition, many tax preparers work at home to earn extra money while they hold a full-time job.

The hours and schedules that tax preparers work vary greatly, depending on the time of year and the manner in which workers are employed. Because of the changes in tax laws that occur every year, tax preparers often advise their clients throughout the year about possible ways to reduce their tax obligations. The first quarter of the year is the busiest time, and even part-time tax preparers may find themselves working very long hours. Workweeks can range from as little as 12 hours to 40 or 50 or more, as tax preparers work late into the evening and on weekends. Tax service firms are usually open seven days a week and 12 hours a day during the first three months of the year. The work is demanding, requiring heavy concentration and long hours sitting at a desk and working on a computer.

OUTLOOK

The U.S. Department of Labor predicts that employment for tax preparers will grow about as fast as the average for all occupations through 2014. According to the IRS, over 50 percent of U.S. taxpayers used paid preparers to file their returns for the 2001 tax year, and because tax laws are constantly changing and growing more complex, demand for tax professionals will remain high. Much of this demand, however, is expected to be met by the tax preparers already working, because computers are increasingly expediting the process of tabulating and storing data. Recent surveys of employers in large metropolitan areas have found an adequate supply of tax preparers; prospects for employment may be better in smaller cities or rural areas.

Although tax laws are constantly evolving and people look to tax preparers to save time, money, and frustration, new tax programs and online resources are easing the process of preparing taxes, lessening the need for outside help. Information is available at the touch of a button on tax laws and regulations. Tax tips are readily available, as are online seminars and workshops.

The IRS currently offers taxpayers and businesses the option to "e-file," or electronically file their tax returns on the Internet. While some people may choose to do their own electronic filing, the majority of taxpayers will still rely on tax preparers—licensed by the IRS as Electronic Return Originators—to handle their returns.

FOR MORE INFORMATION

For information on the certified tax preparer designation, contact
Institute of Tax Consultants
7500 212th SW, Suite 205
Edmonds, WA 98026-7617
Tel: 425-774-3521
http://taxprofessionals.homestead.com/welcome.html

For industry information, contact
National Association of Tax Consultants
PO Box 90276
Portland, OR 97290-0276
Tel: 800-745-6282
http://www.natctax.org

For information on educational programs, publications, and online membership, contact
National Association of Tax Professionals
720 Association Drive
Appleton, WI 54912-8002
Tel: 800-558-3402
Email: natp@natptax.com
http://www.natptax.com

For training programs, contact
H&R Block
http://www.hrblock.com

For information on becoming certified as an enrolled agent, check out the IRS Web site:
Internal Revenue Service
U.S. Department of the Treasury
http://www.irs.ustreas.gov

Index

Entries and page numbers in **bold** indicate major treatment of a topic.